# BEAUTY
## *in the Honey*
### FINDING FREEDOM IN GOD'S GOODNESS

HEIDI HINNENKAMP

# BEAUTY
## in the Honey

### FINDING FREEDOM IN GOD'S GOODNESS

# endorsements

Girlfriend –if you want a life filled with meaning, purpose, and freedom, then join Heidi as she shares her journey of healing, obedience and pressing into God's mercy. Bee forever changed.
*Ruth Buezis*
*Author and Founder of Awaken Love*

Heidi has given us a gift— Insightfully compassionate (from the foreword on, you'll find her heart open and inviting to have you join her in learning about Jesus). Entertainingly informative (you will learn about bees, but also, a spiritual walk, soul care, and experiments of faith). Arrestingly personal (you may find yourself wrestling with concepts unfamiliar, or too familiar, but press on). Powerfully convicting (you will be challenged by her model of openness, encouraged and exhorted by her growing faith). Invitingly hopeful (you may focus on a stronger picture of Jesus and life in Him). Bee Ready!
*Gregory C. Carlson, Ph.D.*
*Professor Emeritus of Christian Ministries and Leadership,*
*Trinity International University*

The older I get, the more I value people who ask tough questions and point out the elephants in the room. As you will see, this raw, rarely-filtered book gives you a window into Heidi's heart and soul as she vulnerably writes truth. I encourage you to journey with Heidi as she shares her story, asks tough questions, and points to answers in God's Word.
*Lisa Dananay*
*Missionary at Camp Forest Springs*

Heidi does a beautiful job revealing God's heart for you while challenging you to examine your heart in every moment of this life with Jesus, even the not-so-fun ones. Beauty in the Honey allows you to have that sister-friend you need in your corner when everything around you is falling apart. She's written this vulnerable encouragement to cheer you on, help you remember, and better see God's truth in your very own life - because it's God's loving truth that heals best.

*Jessica Niroomand-rad*
*Wife and Homeschool Mom*

Beauty in the Honey is beautifully written and Heidi's heart shines through. It felt like I was sitting with Heidi over coffee or tea and sharing our hearts, about what God has done. I absolutely loved each action step and hearing how her story was woven through each chapter and how the Lord shaped her through that with scripture too. It was encouraging to continue to work through what is in my heart and lingering unforgiveness. The Lord wants us to forgive and live free. Reading the whole thing, start to finish, was wonderful but it's also such a great book for when you need reminders, you can go back to a certain chapter and read what you need.

*Kara Larson*
*Pastor's wife and Mom*

# table of contents

Beauty in the Honey: Finding Freedom in God's Goodness
© 2024 Heidi Hinnenkamp

Scriptures taken from the Holy Bible, New International Version®, NIV®. Copyright © 1973, 1978, 1984, 2011 by Biblica, Inc.™ Used by permission of Zondervan. All rights reserved worldwide. www.zondervan.com The "NIV" and "New International Version" are trademarks registered in the United States Patent and Trademark Office by Biblica, Inc.™

Scripture quotations marked (NLT) are taken from the Holy Bible, New Living Translation, copyright © 1996, 2004, 2015 by Tyndale House Foundation. Used by permission of Tyndale House Publishers, Carol Stream, Illinois 60188, USA. All rights reserved.

Heidi Hinnenkamp
beautyinhoney@gmail.com

Cover Design and Layout: Katie Zeliger

Printed in the United States of America
Meraki Press LLC
www.merakipress.org

First Printing, September 2024

*To the women in my life,*
Two sisters, my nieces
Running wild and free with Jesus.
My sister, my oldest friend
Love that runs deep to the end.
All kindred sisters, my hope and dream
For wild hearts to be set free.

# *introduction*

Hi friend,

You know when you're going through a difficult season and you wish someone would read between the lines to notice your pain? You're walking through a desert season of loneliness or the pain is paralyzing, and you can't verbalize why you are crying or what is knotting you up inside. You don't know what you are feeling, and you wish your husband or a friend would just know what you're feeling without you having to say. There is a story behind the tears, an ocean of anguish you can't put words to. It's easy to eat a spoonful of sweet honey, but it is not just the honey on the spoon. There are thousands of bees working behind the scenes producing the honey, day and night faithfully building the comb, bringing in the pollen from the fields, fanning out the moisture to the perfect eighteen percent before capping. And when you see beyond the honey to the quiet work behind the scenes, that honey becomes a work of art, a thing of beauty. That's what this book is about—a real story behind the story. God, in His goodness, is quietly working in the background of our lives and bringing purpose to our pain and tears. My prayer is that your heart is ready and willing to see beyond the surface to the deeper meaning behind the tears and peel away the layers to the deeper truth of Jesus, as Paul says it in Ephesians 1:18 NLT, "may the eyes of your heart be flooded with light so that you can understand the confident hope he has given to those he called—his holy people who are his rich and glorious inheritance." We are asked to have faith like children and let our hearts be open to the Lord's teaching.

When I was younger, I felt like a bird trapped in a cage and wished I could live in the sunshine, wild and free. I limped along with a broken wing and a gloomy mood for a long time until I really saw the truth of Jesus for myself, and the truth set me free (John 8:31-32 NLT). There is a

God who wants to set us free. I don't pretend to know the pain you carry or the road you have walked, and I certainly don't have all the perfect answers, but I do know God wants you to be a woman who lives wild and free. The Lord is good, and He doesn't want us to live in bondage or be hindered by a broken wing. "Taste and see the Lord is good; blessed is the one who takes refuge in Him" (Psalm 34:8 NLT). There is more beyond the surface of simply believing and hopefully my story will point you to the One who can heal your broken wing as you walk out these action steps.

We all carry wounds on our own journey back to Eden, the garden of perfection where we will walk with Jesus again—the garden of Eden where trees are lush, the violets are deep hues of purples, and the vibrant colors of the rainbow are all around. The fruit tastes sweeter than our palette has ever experienced, and bees are quietly working in the background as our senses are heightened to the brilliance of our surroundings. We can look forward to that day, but while we have breath in our lungs, we are sojourners on a tangled road and our wounds can feel too raw to face. We can believe Jesus died on the cross to set us free, but we have the choice to be reborn in Christ and let Him heal our wounds. We can choose to confront some of our wounds in the silent sufferings of our journal, some we are forced to face in the agony of a sudden loss, while others bubble to the surface in the isolation of a desert season. We can let Jesus be our comforter and friend, fulfilling all our needs as we all face the same choice every day to lay those burdens at the cross and find freedom. We can try to take an easier path around the pain and bypass the hard road, but the reward is revealed when we surrender to what the Lord is teaching. We may think how could this possibly be God's will to go the hard way, but it may be exactly His will for you to walk through the tangles, wholly relying on Him alone and simply trusting His guiding hand. There will be seasons when it feels like no one is coming to your rescue and you realize you're on your own island, and you could be exactly where God wants you to be. So often we want to avoid the pain, cry out for rescue, desperate for someone to hear, but surrendering to the hard road leads us to the greatest reward, digging up the hard soil yields the sweetest fruit, and having the courage to wait on the Lord's timing brings us to the best gift.

We are to simply trust our Savior Jesus in those seasons and choose to come to the cross in surrender. Jesus in his humanity didn't want to drink the cup of wrath; He asked the Father if there was another way, but he surrendered to the Father's will, and it was good. The process doesn't always feel good in the moment, but the fruit revealed is worth it. He is worthy of our praise. He alone is our safe refuge. "THIS I declare about the Lord, He alone is my refuge, my place of safety; he is my God and I trust him" (Psalm 91:2 NLT). In those seasons, when He is bringing us through the darkest valley (Psalm 23:4 NLT), are we fearing evil or are we holding his gentle hand and letting Him lead the way?

I love jumping into the tangles with a friend who is ready and willing to share her heart. My husband, Sam, can tell you on our first date I went straight to pecking at the walls of his heart by asking deep questions. I can be a strong-headed woodpecker who pecks and pecks, and it can come across as intense, but I have come to learn God made me in His image and a certain way for His purposes. He has made you for a purpose and brought you to a place where you can find healing and freedom, if you choose. I want to walk with you and show you there is a way out. I can be a friend here while we journey through this book, but I encourage you to let the Holy Spirit guide you out of your tangles. Let the mercy of God and insights open up to you as you walk forward in faith, and little by little, the path will become clear. We find Jesus is by our side the whole time. He has never left.

I love the Lord with all my heart and my faith has grown deeper and my maturity strengthened, but this is not your typical feel-good, faith-based book. You are here because you know there is more to this God—you hunger and thirst for more of Him, but you can't seem to push past what feels like a tangled mess and grow deeper in your relationship. You are doing all the so-called "right" things but feel stuck and can't seem to ever break free. Maybe you faithfully go to church every week and sit in your seat hoping for some miraculous transformation to happen. The Church tells us we are free in Christ, right? So why aren't we truly free? God has a message sweet as honey to speak to your heart, and if you are ready and willing to look beyond the surface to deeper depths, you will find a treasure more beautiful than your present pain can comprehend. I am not here to tell you what your itching ears want to hear (2 Timothy 4:3 NLT); I want to get to the depth and truth of God, and I will peck until we find the treasure.

Maybe that sounds impossible. Maybe God has disappointed you and you were about to close this book and throw it across the room but hold on to that thread of hope a little longer. I know what it is like living in the shadows, being overlooked, being teased, and being rejected by relationships. I have walked through valleys of loneliness so dark that it hurts and gone so deep into the caverns of my own mind that it is tormenting. The Lord was allowing these trials and rocks on the road to strengthen my mind and purify my heart so I could see more outside of myself to the grander story He designed. Pain has many faces, and Jesus was sent to comfort us in our pain. He came to set us free from that bondage so we wouldn't have to suffer our whole lives. We can get entangled in lies and deceptions, stuck in our own suffering and selfishness, but I know God plants us in this culture, this town, at this time of history for the purpose of loving Him and making His name known.

This is not my story to be told, but the story God has been writing all along in every chapter of my life. I genuinely believe He wants you to hear it. I write this in fear and trembling; I am a simple homeschool mom to six little ones here to share a story of both the pruning of dead branches and the blooming of fruit. I can share what I have learned, and pray you allow the Holy Spirit to reveal the deeper layers in your own heart. I hope I can be a friend in some small way, and if we ever meet, we could become fast friends. I am willing to be an open book if that means a friend will catch a glimpse of Jesus and discover the treasure of seeing more of the goodness of God. As the bees buzz in the garden and stillness is in the air, we find God there. The beauty and the sweetness are found in the journey, in the stillness. I happen to be a beekeeper, but my love for bees did not start in a garden or in tasting the sweet honey. The life of the honeybee has been many lessons buzzing in the background all throughout my life long before I ever caught my first wild swarm. We can rest and be at ease knowing God is the Author. He wrote the whole story from the beginning with Adam to the end of Revelation with the second coming of Christ. He knows every detail that is happening in our world, and He knows every detail of your intricate, beautifully complicated heart.

We were made to praise the name of the Lord (Psalm 19 NLT) to live in abundant joy and thank Him in all things. He longs for us to notice Him, to taste and see His goodness (Psalm 34:8 NLT) and bloom into the women He made us to be. We serve a big God who can do infinitely more than we can imagine, and He is more intimately involved in the details of our lives than we can fathom. "He is mightier than the violent raging of the seas, mightier than the breakers on the shore – the Lord is mightier than these" (Psalm 93:4 NLT). We serve the God who has the burning ardor to meet you in your every need and calm the raging seas in your heart. He longs to set you free.

All He asks is that you *Bee* Still with Him and rest, the Lord is by your side.


With love,
Heidi Hinnenkamp

# chapter 1

Millie the bee had miraculously survived the long journey through the postal service to our doorstep. Our swarm trap package of beekeeping supplies had arrived with our jackets and hats, tools, and swarm trap box. As we tore through all the bubble wrap, my kids giggled with glee. It wasn't until I began cleaning up the mess that I noticed a bit of black fuzz. I was about to vacuum it up when it started moving.

I could not believe what I was seeing. A little honeybee was walking on my kitchen floor. This sweet little bee had found her way into the box and not only survived the shipping journey, but survived the frenzy of unboxing with my five little fireball children. We swooned over that sweet bee as if a new baby had been announced.

Of course, my daughter wanted to name her and declared Millie was her name.

I giggled. "Yes, sweet daughter, Millie is perfect."

We made a home for Millie. We put her on a playset tea plate with a tiny teacup of water and a drop of honey on the side. She was away from her colony, alone on this grand adventure, and we assumed she must have been thirsty from her long journey. We watched little Millie for over an hour as she lapped up the honey and explored her surroundings. Then, we made up a warm home of flowers in a vase. She was away from the safety and protection of the hive, and we couldn't just release her outside to be exposed to the elements. We made a comfortable place for the night and put her into a warm sunflower bed the next morning.

Millie's presence felt like a gift, and we were smitten.

It may seem silly to take notice of one tiny bee, but it was a miraculous moment to us. We were witnessing the resiliency of this honeybee to survive. Deep in my heart I knew this was the first of many lessons in our days of beekeeping on our little farm.

God offers us gifts every day. He presents opportunities to teach us. It is our choice to either notice those opportunities, or let them buzz on by. We could have taken Millie outside immediately and found a flower in our garden, instead we slowed down and savored the moment.

When I first became interested in beekeeping and researching all the different methods, I had a few seasoned beekeepers discourage me from swarm catching in our first year. They would tell me catching a swarm of wild bees in our own trap was not for new beekeepers and chances of catching any bees was very unlikely. They suggested I purchase a package or a colony of bees from a local beekeeper. The more we questioned and searched for the best way, the more we realized what bees naturally do in nature is the best way. It was the same realization when selecting which method to use. There are several methods of keeping bees and every beekeeper I met seemed to use the Langstroth method, a style that uses stacked boxes. I couldn't make sense of how that method worked best for the bees, and it seemed too complicated for me to understand how to manage the bees. These beekeepers were encountering the same issues and the same vicious cycle every year of combating pests and diseases. They were purchasing a colony of 20,000+ bees that were being shipped to them in the mail from another beekeeper, then transferring the bees to their box and having to protect against different pests, and in many cases, the bees weren't staying in the box. The Langstroth method seemed to require more steps to maintain the bees and shifting the different boxes made the bees more vulnerable to the elements. It was mentioned more than once how often swarms were lost or colonies died in their first year, and that was after they had spent hundreds of dollars getting colonies of bees shipped to them. It seemed too big a monetary risk and I thought what was the harm in putting up a swarm trap? If I didn't attract any bees to our garden we could try again the next season, and if bees did come, what an amazing miracle to be a part of.

Then we came across the Layens Hive method and everything about this method made the most sense to me. It seemed most in line with God's design. It was a simple box with a row of frames and plenty of room for the bees to build out their honeycomb foundation. Georges De Layens was a botanist and an apiculturist in the 1800's, and he came up with this method that was most natural to how bees function in nature. We were being discouraged in the choice to venture into natural beekeeping as well.

I asked the question at a beekeeping workshop if any of the instructors up front do natural beekeeping and the response came with an emphatic "Ha! Good luck with that! We had someone ask that question last year and do you see that lady here this year?" I was stunned and speechless, clearly it was not the workshop for me to get the support I was looking for. I had resolved in my heart to be still and surrender to God's plan for creation, letting whatever happens that first year to happen naturally. I was going to enjoy the entire process from start to finish, not just manipulate the parts I wanted for convenience or skip the parts that were hard. If it was a slow first year or a scout bee never found our swarm box, I would be ok with that. I wanted to experience every step, every birth pang, and learn from every struggle along the way. I was going to put up a swarm trap in a tree and see what happened. In the stillness, I could hear the gentle voice of God sharing a lesson and I wasn't going to miss it. He was teaching me there is beauty in the process and as we press in and slowly peel back the layers, He reveals more of His truth. He opens the eyes of our hearts and enables us to see more clearly who He is and His perspective. So often, we want to skip the process and jump to the end or manipulate the process and make it faster. We want the honey harvest but we may miss all the glory God wants to show us and His peaceful presence along the way.

Sure enough, God showed us His glory in abundance that first year. He showed us His way in creation is the best, most beautiful way. We were out in the yard when my husband, Sam heard a loud buzzing sound and started to look around. He spotted a black cloud headed toward our bee yard and started screaming across the property to go look. It was an exceptionally large colony and I got to witness the majestic moment of the thousands of bees marching into the box, as the guard bees "stood" watch on both sides of the entrance. I stood there in amazement with a few runaway tears trailing down my face. It was nothing short of a miracle. That colony continued to thrive and grow over the next few seasons. We were able to split the hive multiple times and help four new beekeepers on their journey. The honey harvest produced was more than we could have imagined. We have caught and lost colonies along the way as well, but every time we slowed down the process, God met us there. He says, "Be still and know that I am God" (Psalm 46:10a NLT).

We see nature's example of this in many areas. Think about baby chicks, for instance. They have to peck around the whole eggshell on their own or they will die. If we crack the shell for them and rush the process, they won't thrive. We can't give numbing drops to ease their struggle. The struggle is what gives them the strength they need to survive those first days.

When we yield to the process of our struggle, we will eventually experience the reward. There will be obstacles in every journey, but we must break through if we want to get to the other side. We can't go over the wall and skip the pain, we can't go around the wall and bypass the struggle, we have to go through, or we will never experience the beauty of breakthrough.

We have to be willing to do the work, a word we don't always like to hear. Personal work and allowing the Lord to work on our hearts is actually really wonderful if we are willing to be humbled and learn along the way.

If we look at nature, we see there is a buildup to every majesty, a climax to every sound, an ecstasy to every aspect of creation. A sunrise is a slow buildup, and we experience the bursting majesty of the sun rays coming up over the horizon. The blazing sun in the sky is the end reward, but watching it burst is the gift. The climax is the gift, we find the climax and the ecstasy in the process.

The ecstasy of creation can be found in spending hours watching a chick hatch her way out or taking the time to watch a lone honeybee after a long journey. When we listen to the waves rhythmically crash into shore as the sun rises, or pause to feel the breeze bustling through the palm trees, there is boundless joy. We can watch birds swoop down for their breakfast, or we can spot a dolphin pop up to the surface. As we are watching, waiting, and embracing the process, we are experiencing the true gift.

It is in the stillness that we find the gift.

We will never experience the real gift of joy without surrendering to the process.

We can accept these gifts along the way or skip right over them.

My interest in beekeeping did not start out with an appreciation for the honeybee. I never had the dream to one day live on a farm and keep bees. My love for bees started in a way I least expected. I left home at eighteen years old and set off for college, striving for a dream that felt attainable. It was a good dream and seemed well intentioned. I was going to become a nurse, meet a man in ministry school, marry him, and together we would go on the mission field for the wildest adventure of our lives. I grew up listening to missionaries speak from all over the world, hearing their stories of following God's will. It sounded so exciting to me! I heard about churches being planted in remote areas of the world and ministries blossoming, I heard of the Good News being spread, lives being radically transformed and families overcoming impossible circumstances. I sat on the edge of my seat, soaking in every word of these powerful stories, hearing about a mighty God who could work miracles out of nothing.

I had built up the Christian journey in my own mind to be a glamorous life of doing important work for God and I had my steps all mapped out ready to strive after this grand dream. It felt within reach if I just tried harder or studied more, but with every step, reality was teaching me the opposite was true. I was learning a hard lesson in stillness – that my plans were not God's plans. When we decide to follow Jesus, we must realize our life is not our own – this is a truth that was going to take me a long time to fully understand. God was gently beginning to teach me the word "surrender" little by little. As I was striving after my own plans and fairy-tale dreams, God was teaching me to be still and seek Him.

In stillness we find peace and we are reminded God is God and we are not. He reveals which way to go and gives us the answers we seek to find, as long as we seek His kingdom first and go back to what the Bible teaches.

David cries out the song of his heart in Psalm 46 (NLT). He doesn't hold back his praise when facing trials. "God is our refuge and strength, always ready to help in times of trouble." When trials come, when our world falls apart, we don't have to fear. When the mountains crumble into the sea, we don't have to be afraid. This song of praise is in the Bible for a reason. It was to prepare us in advance for the trials we would face. David goes on to say "Let the oceans roar and foam. Let the mountains tremble as the waters surge!" He said, "Let them!"

The trials will come. Jesus said in the gospel of John that we will face trials of many kinds in this life, but He didn't say we would face them with no hope in sight. He said to cheer up, because He has overcome it all. He already won the victory, and we can live today rejoicing in the good news. Bad news may hit us in the face and shatter the ground we walk on, but when we go back to our secret place in the stillness, we find our breath again. He comforts us and brings us peace.

Psalm 46 goes on singing, "A river brings joy to the city of our God, the sacred home of the Most High. God dwells in the city; it cannot be destroyed. From the very break of day, God will protect it. The nations are in chaos, and their kingdoms crumble!" Did you hear that? When our world is in chaos and kingdoms are crumbling, God is still there. He promised He would never leave or forsake us. Even when we are walking through a valley we will get to the other side and see that He was there the whole time. He may even have a purpose we can't see yet.

"God's voice thunders and the earth melts. The Lord of heaven's Armies is here among us; the God of Israel is our fortress." God is among us. He is in the mess, in the tangles. He is the beauty among the thorns. "Come, see the glorious works of the Lord; See how he brings destruction upon the world. He causes wars to end throughout the earth. He breaks the bows and snaps the spears; He burns the shields with fire.

"Be still and know I am God!

"I will be honored by every nation; I will be honored throughout the world. The Lord of heaven's Armies is here among us; the God of Israel is our fortress."

When God tells us to be still it is because He has something to say. He wants us to hear Him and pay close attention to what follows. I imagine Him slowing the earth's spin on its axis to a standstill and tenderly holding my face in His hands to quietly speak, saying "Rest my girl, slow down and pause. I make the seasons so you will notice the stillness in dormancy, press into the moment and be with Me." He longs for us to be with Him, to walk with Him and talk with Him. He is sauntering through the garden, savoring each step, enjoying each moment. In those true moments of stillness with Him, we notice a bee buzzing or feel the breeze on our skin, we feel most alive when we are wrapped up with Him. He wants us to stop striving and just be.

Sometimes as a daughter, we need to be held and corrected by a loving Father. In my young years, I had a very stubborn heart. I wasn't learning and I wasn't letting God correct me. I was striving to please Him and seeking approval. In the constant striving, I found myself on a very painful, very broken path. I didn't know how to find my way back. My stubborn heart needed firm correction and God, in His steadfast kindness, continually taught me to be still. At times, he firmly told me to just *bee* and stop striving.

God never got impatient with me, and He won't with you either. But He does correct those He loves (Proverbs 3:11 NLT). At first, I didn't see Him as a kind heavenly Father who was after my heart. He was going to punish me or judge me if I didn't do an important job for Him. I often wondered if I would ever be enough. I was striving to be important and to be noticed. I was afraid of falling short. I didn't know it then, but I can see it now. He wanted me to cease striving after attention and just be with Him. I call those six years of college "the thorny years," but out of that time, beauty still found a way to sprout.

I had a college professor that told me I was "in the blooming process," and little did I know how profound those words would be in shaping my life. It was six years filled with raw and painful emotions. I was walking through a jungle that seemed to only get more tangled the further I walked, and I was making a mess of things. I was doing everything I thought I needed to do and, in the process, facing many dead ends. I kept getting caught up in a whirl of distractions and chaos.

We all make mistakes along the way, but in this season the Lord was gently telling me to slow down, breathe, and listen to His words. The world may swirl around us, but we can find stillness right in the midst of it if we look to Jesus. If we're sitting by the river listening to the steady trickle of waters passing by, we can notice the tiny flower slightly swaying in the breeze. There is a comfort, a peace in watching that little flower – knowing God cares about that tiny flower in full bloom. That may read as a corny Christian truth, but it's true. He made that flower grow from seed and He made you to be a woman blooming. God created you and cares about you. He won't leave you.

If you have been a Christ follower for any amount of time, you likely know the simple song "Jesus loves you," but hear me, the simple truth is we find God, and feel His love, in the stillness. The more we learn to slow down, be still, go to that secret place and turn our eyes to Jesus, the more He settles the storms inside of us. The world can seem like a tornado, but in the quiet, secret place of prayer, He can stop our spinning.

We can experience a peace in His presence that is beyond any logic. When people are running around in total pandemonium, we can be at total peace, unruffled, and unphased knowing God has it under control. Jesus taught us through his daily rhythms to go away to the secret place. He went away every day to be with the Father. It wasn't His religious duty; it was to be with the Father.

We have access to the Father through Jesus, to be with the One we love. It isn't our daily duty; it is to spend time in relationship with our Father God. In this secret place of prayer, we allow Him to calm our hearts and rest our minds. We can savor the minutes in His presence and be so enraptured in the moment, we don't want to be anywhere else. This secret place is special because it's where we can freely praise the God who made us. God is worthy to be praised simply because of who He is.

He made us to be in His presence. He wants to know you intimately and speak tenderly to you there. So often we want to rush ahead, but God speaks to our heart, "No, not yet, dear one, just *bee*." When I refused to be still with God, I found that all my plans seemed to fail. Door after door would close. It would seem all my efforts were never enough time and time again. The Lord was trying to teach me to slow down and turn my eyes back to Jesus, surrendering my plans to Him.

There may be thorns and difficulties in your life, but there is still so much to be thankful for and if we're willing to walk in faith through those thorns, then God will never cease to amaze us with what gifts He wants to share with us. It is so hard for us to rest and be still. It is not in our human nature to enjoy the simple pleasures or notice the little flowers in our path. Oftentimes, we may feel overlooked, so we struggle and strive to succeed. We want to control our circumstances and rush ahead to make things happen.

Something in us hungers for more, but we don't realize we were made to know more of God. The secret to knowing God's will can seem complicated but it is as simple as child-like faith. He wants us to know Him and to love Him with all our heart. He wants us to choose Him. When we finally relent and let our guard down, He can come to us and show us more of Himself. We want to skip ahead to the end result and bypass everything in between; the lessons, the buildup, the trials, the pain, the climax, the ecstasy, and the poetry. But if we do that, we end up completely missing the treasures in the struggle.

If we slow down and notice our surroundings, we will see all around us is an awe-inspiring, emotional experience. It is a symphony of music to our ears, painted with the grandest landscapes, splashed with the deepest, most vast oceans, filled with animals of wondrous creation. It is beyond what our wildest imagination could dream up.

There is a song unfolding in every note around us. From the tiniest detail of mushrooms that grow in the soggy ground, all the way to the explosion of summer cicadas' chorus during sunset. If we make the effort to wake up before dawn to see and experience an ocean view sunrise, we are reminded of how small we are in the grander design of creation.

In the midst of my efforts to race ahead, God was ever so patiently teaching me to slow down and be present in the journey so I wouldn't miss a moment. He made us to walk with Him in the garden, converse with Him and know Him. That is who He made you to be, a woman who loves the Lord with all her heart, all her soul, all her mind, and all her strength

(Mark 12:30 NLT). When you begin to grasp that love, you will want to please Him, but you will find yourself not striving anymore. The will to fight will leave and the storm will settle.

He just wants you. He wants your heart.

"The Lord will fight for you; you need only to be still" (Exodus 14:14 NIV).

Though your heart may be broken with the pain of sin and the struggles of our fallen world, His love for you is not broken. The pain and brokenness you feel is tied back to the very beginning when Adam and Eve broke the relationship with God, our Creator. He has a plan to restore that brokenness. He has a plan to restore that simple, beautiful union in all its purity. He invites us to slow down and be active participants in creation with Him as he heals us. As I sit here sipping my last drop of white pumpkin mocha, the stillness can feel lonely, but I am not alone. God is in the quiet with me, giving me courage to stay and wait upon him as He heals me.

What is one way you can slow down today long enough to tune your heart into the quiet sounds? Write down what you hear.

Do you fear the quiet and stillness?

How have you heard the voice of God in the stillness?

What brings stillness to your soul?

Where is your quiet place?

**Let's put our faith into action and take one step. Action Step #1.**

Buy yourself a journal. Write the words "Notice Notebook" on the front and decorate it in a way that brings you joy. Let that journal be a companion on this road the Lord is bringing you on. It's okay if you don't enjoy journaling or even writing. The point of this journal is to go to your quiet place, set a timer if that helps, and notice something new in your day. Write it down, draw it. Scribble a blob if nothing comes to mind. The simple action step will set your mind on new pathways. You set the number of days you are going to commit to doing this. Ask the Lord if there is a certain number. This may feel awkward to pray at first, but He will meet you in that place of obedience if you stick to the commitment.

# BEE STILL

HOW MANY DAYS AM I GOING TO START
MY DAY PRACTICING BEING STILL?

1 DAY     2 DAYS     3 DAYS     4 DAYS     5 DAYS

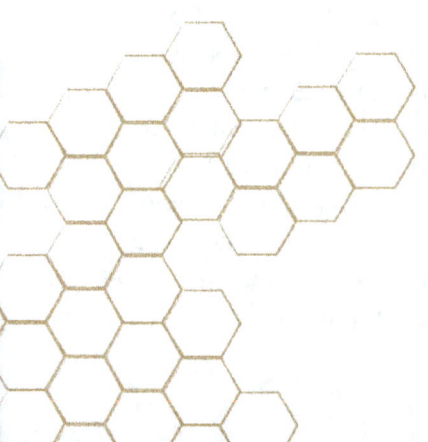

This little bee accidentally got squashed between two frames and I watched as she slowly stumbled along and drank her last meal. In the stillness of the garden, I was reminded of the value of life. Every life matters.

# chapter 2

It was six "thorny years" of college. Six long years when Satan was working hard to thwart God's plans for me. I wasn't pursuing the heart of God or His path for my life. I was so sure, so confident I already knew the path He had set for me, and I was racing ahead, but I was just chasing the wind. I was a teenager talking to everyone with boldness about this wild, exciting plan I was pursuing. I went into those years starry eyed, ready to get my nursing degree, marry my ministry man, and discover this important purpose God was going to give me. Instead, they were years Satan found my weak spot and tangled me up.

Our enemy, Satan, sets his own plans in motion to distract us, to make us question our worth, and strike at our confidence. He was planting thorny weeds in my path, and I was letting them trip me up. I was falling right into his deceptions and did not even fight back. My heart was not paying attention to God's promptings at every point along the path. I blazed right on by, ignoring His warnings.

I was living a double life – professing to be a Christ-follower while living in blatant sin. My first two years in nursing school were one disappointment after another, like blowing a cloud of bubbles and popping each one as they floated to the ground. I was failing my classes, falling behind, and letting everyone down back home. I was the definition of a self-righteous hypocrite, sleeping over with boyfriends but never crossing the technical line. The thorns in my heart were growing thick and they were doing more damage than I could grasp. I had wise mentors warning me of the consequences of my sin, but I didn't listen. By the end of my second year of nursing school, my dream was shattered. I allowed sin to take over and eat away at me, distracting me from my studies and I flunked out of the program. My confidence was shaken. I had to face the shame and move back home.

The self-seeking sin continued to take root. We cannot fool ourselves into believing any form of sexuality outside of God's design is acceptable. Sin will continue to slowly erode our hearts. I was a tangled mess of confusion and couldn't focus on anything. I turned to alcohol in secret and soaked in the attention from guys to silence my thoughts. God's mercy was holding my hand every step of the way, even when I was not holding onto His. He was gently bringing me back to stillness.

When I was living back at home, the Lord was chipping away at the prideful dream I had clung so tightly to. He was humbling me and setting me on a new path. I was driving to a community college every day and in my commute, the confidence in self I had built up was slowly being knocked down. The nursing school path took a detour, and I was working with people with disabilities. Suddenly it wasn't about my selfish desires anymore. I found myself serving and loving a population that were angels of this earth, but it still felt like a detour from my original plans. I was confident I would get back to nursing school and go on with my grand pursuit. The Lord had different plans, but I was still not listening. I was fighting inner turmoil, and the man I had been intimately involved with for two years had enough of the tug of war and walked away. I was left shattered and heartbroken. The sin struggle did not disappear, it only deepened. I entered my third college, still wholeheartedly believing God's will for me was to go on the mission field. I was humbled and let go of my aspirations to be a nurse. I would continue to pursue the social services path and see if that took me where I wanted to go. I was at a ministry school, one that brought seminary students from all over the world, and it was right down the road from home. I was even more sure, more confident this must be the plan God had for me. There is no path we take, no mistake we make that goes to waste, but God was still waiting for me to stop striving and come to Him and rest. He is long-suffering and waits patiently for us. He is not going to force us to slow down and listen, but He will use trials, heartaches, and detours to call our name until we hear His gentle voice. Confidence in self is always going to shatter. He was tenderly redirecting me to put my confidence in Him.

The sin struggle felt even more intense being at a ministry school where we were studying to be pastors and leaders in churches. But the truth is, sexual sin rears its ugly head in many facets. I wore my purity ring proudly, telling myself my sexual sin was ok because I was a Christ-follower at ministry school, and I wouldn't cross the line. I was certain the man I was dating was the man I was going to marry. People know the first moment they meet, right? I knew – I thought I knew. My heartstrings were knotted up tightly in him and I was not going to let him go. I was chest deep committed and with every argument, it was just a matter of working through it and trying harder. He was going to be a pastor and had a big heart for mission work. We traveled the world together and I was fully convinced, hand in hand, we could face anything. He was the love of my life. In the end, we got off one flight and went two separate ways, never to hold hands again. My confidence was completely shattered, and God was finally getting my attention.

The finish line of graduation was in sight, I had one year left, and my heart finally surrendered to hearing His voice. I spent that year in intimate silence with Him, learning from His Word and listening to His direction. I still had to see the man my soul was tied to every day around campus, as he walked hand in hand with his fiancé, but the Lord was recapturing my heart. It was a year filled with cleansing tears and healing. I was savoring the stillness and felt free in my commitment to stay single, but I was still aimless. I felt like a slave to my sin struggle and ministry school added more chaos to my confusion with all the knowledge and debates being crammed in my head. I was held captive in the prison of my own mind. Those years left me uncertain on which way to go next and I needed help, I needed a Rescuer.

We can force our plans to work and we can be devastated when they don't, but God's ways are higher than our ways. He was using every bit of the mess I made and began weaving something beautiful in the background. Just like my beloved bees busy in the background, faithfully bringing in the pollen, fanning the moisture to a perfect eighteen percent and capping the honey with their intricately designed wax. We don't always slow down long enough to notice the honeybee, but they are there, diligently working the task that is in front of them.

God was revealing how my self-confidence was misplaced and not only teaching me to discern truth from lies about myself, but also teaching me to discern truth from lies in the world. We make our plans and set goals to achieve success, yet rarely do we pause to ask God if it is the path He wants us to take. We fall into these traps and believe lies the world tells us, even follow the logic of our own minds. The word "truth" can make some people cringe. We hear "Live your truth," your truth is your truth, right? It is a word that is shoved in our faces in the media, online, even in the grocery store. But for the purpose of these pages, we need to learn to silence the lies and listen to the only truth; the truth we find in scripture. We can grow in confidence that what the Lord is showing us is actually true. Scripture says to be alert, to be aware of the signs of our times. We can't hide behind lies or waste time plugging our ears to the truth. We can come out of that darkness and rediscover the truth of who God says we are as women, as children of God, daughters of the Most High, our heavenly Father. There is confidence we find when God reveals that truth. We can turn our thoughts to good things, fixing our thoughts on what is true, honorable, right, pure, lovely, and admirable, thinking on things that are excellent and worthy of praise (Phil. 4:8 NLT). We can be confident He will lead us where He wants us to go.

The Israelites were slaves in captivity for over 400 years and Pharaoh was not going to let them go. They needed a Rescuer and God sent them one. Moses was sent as a baby to Egypt and lived among his people for forty years, he spent the next forty years running away in the desert before God got his attention and sent him back to Egypt to lead his people out of slavery. It took eighty years for his heart to be ready and willing to obey, but God in His long-suffering didn't give up on the good plan for His people.

For those eighty years, the Jews were held captive in slavery under Pharaoh and Moses was there in the background, being prepared to rescue them. They didn't see the work God was doing or the preparation in the background. God was working for their good in what most likely felt like dead silence for decades, but His glory would be on display soon. They had to keep trusting in the silence and waiting. When Moses came to lead them out, Pharaoh would not allow his slaves to be set free. God performed many miracles by sending ten plagues to stir up Pharaoh, but his heart was still hardened. It wasn't until he lost his firstborn son that he finally relented and let the people go. Moses led the people out of captivity into the wilderness.

So often we build our confidence in "self," we lean on our own understanding, rather than trusting that God's leading is safe and secure to follow. Imagine the fear and trepidation the Israelites may have felt as they stood at the Red Sea. They were surrounded. The water's edge was ahead of them and their captors were closing in behind. All they had ever known was the brutal mistreatment by their Egyptian captors and their logic was telling them there was no way out of this torment. But God. He made a way. Moses was told to put his staff in the water and instantly the seas split, paving a way down the middle for God's people to walk. They had to take a step of faith and trust Moses' leadership. They had to trust God's miracle was going to safely bring them to the other side. They spent the next forty years wandering and doubting God's goodness, but Moses' confidence did not rest in his own logic and understanding, he had faith God would show them the way into the Promised Land. He trusted God at every step along the way as provisions were sent daily from heaven.

We have the choice to wander aimlessly, going our own way and striving after our own plans. God won't force us to follow Him. He didn't force the Israelites to trust His mysterious ways. Even after all the miracles performed to bring them out of captivity and provide for them all those years in the desert, many didn't follow and Moses didn't live to see the day they entered the Promised Land. He passed the torch to Joshua to lead the few who stayed faithful and true. God's ways are not our ways, and we must be willing to slow down and seek Him to find Him.

When I finally surrendered to God's ways and tuned into hearing His voice, that is when my childhood friend came back into my life. He became my best friend. He pointed my sail toward the One who could truly heal me and lead me out of sin. We got married a few months later and he stuck by my side on the arduous road to healing. We dreamt of leaving the American lifestyle behind and serving God in another country. But instead of the grand missionary aspirations to an African village, once again God was continuing to humble me with His plans.

Do you enjoy putting together puzzles?

Where can you see glimpses of the puzzle God is piecing together in your life?

How have those seasons of suffering had a purpose?

**Action step #2.**
Take a trip to a thrift store (I would definitely be joining you on this adventure!!) and pick out a puzzle. I hate thousand-piece puzzles and tend to complete the border before putting it back in the box. Maybe you hate puzzles altogether, so get a hundred-piece puzzle. The point is to pause. In those moments of pause, ponder what is true, what is lovely, and listen to what the Lord is saying. Once you complete the project, take one piece of the puzzle, and trace it in your Notice Notebook. Let it serve as

a reminder that you are taking steps of faith toward personal victory and growing more in your confidence in the Lord. Write down the Bible verse Philippians 4:8 and look beyond the one puzzle piece to the bigger picture, as if standing on a mountain looking down on the city. God is piecing the picture together and it is a masterpiece, you will see.

"Finally, brothers and sisters, whatever is true, whatever is noble, whatever is right, whatever is pure, whatever is lovely, whatever is admirable—if anything is excellent or praiseworthy—think about such things." (Philippians 4:8 NLT)

# L*VELY

*noble*

**TRUE**

**RIGHT**

*pure*

## WHAT IS THE PICTURE ON YOUR PUZZLE PIECE?

# chapter 3

When it's my pick for movie night, I always have a true story queued up and our stash of snacks pulled out from the closet. Some movies leave me feeling emboldened and filled with courage; while other stories leave me feeling deep sadness and conviction. Watching the brutality humans endure or the suffering they survive leaves me with a feeling of utter brokenness and deep conviction. In a small way, their suffering reminds me of my own and what Christ suffered for us. It is beyond our comprehension how we are able to survive the pain we as humans can inflict on others. Whether we know it or not, we are all wounded. We carry scars from every relationship, every breakup, every sibling battle, and parental downfall. We will carry those wounds and be tormented by them until we relent and seek forgiveness. God, the Father, invites us to lay our wounds down at the foot of the cross and accept the sacrifice that Christ paid for our healing.

If you have been in the church for any time, "at the foot of the cross" can sound like an overused statement that tends to lose its meaning. It is one piece of the puzzle, and "Leave your burdens at the foot of the cross," can sound like a nice way to tie up a sermon. If we do not truly understand what these statements mean then we are left to carry home the same heavy baggage we brought with us to church. Sometimes we don't even realize the effects our wounds and burdens have on our daily lives. They can be a subtle undercurrent, like television fuzz playing in the background or like seeds strategically planted by the enemy and slowly taking root long before we realized they had power over us.

My heart was left in my birthplace, South Africa, after spending time there in college. I was longing to leave the American lifestyle behind. While mine and my husband's sight was set on mission work to an African village, God was unfolding a much bigger story than we could see. He was pursuing our hearts and confronting that "television fuzz" that was hindering us. We were just a tiny piece of the puzzle. He gave us a child – then four more – and moved us all around. I was still clinging tight to the grand purpose of missions as we were searching for an open door and trying to be faithful in the waiting, but I had a stubborn heart and there was still work to be done.

We did not realize God had quite a different plan for us than we thought. Once again He brought us back to the verse: "Be still and know I am God," (Psalm 46:10 NLT). Once again He reminded us to stop striving. He had a plan all along to untangle the knots of sin and show us the truth of what it meant to drop our burdens at the cross. We were coming face to face with our demons and confronting the baggage we brought into marriage. We were never ready for any mission field. God was after our hearts and in His goodness, He was protecting us from the glamorous purpose we had fabricated in our own imagination. He had a plan to teach us the true gospel, to shepherd us to green pastures and lead us by still waters (Psalm 23:2 NLT). He was revealing the truth behind the veil. It wasn't a quick process, but slowly, gently, and through some distressing experiences in churches, He was giving us glimpses of His plan for the Church and our role in the body of believers. It was beginning to unfold for us. His plan for His children and what was being revealed was quite exquisite.

While our spirit is willing and desires to be set free from heavy burdens, our flesh fights against surrender. Deep in our souls, we have selfishness and pride that wants to hold onto our wounds. Our flesh doesn't want to let go of the burdens we have grown comfortable having around. Pain can deceive us. We feel justified by holding onto our pain. We believe we were hurt, and we want the one who inflicted the pain to know what they've done. We think if we hold onto it, we aren't letting them get away with it. But all that really does is make us bitter and the "fuzz" to grow louder. It becomes a part of who we are, our DNA becomes rewritten, and we believe it is normal. To confront it would mean admitting we have been wrong or deceived and that is too big to face. But God always instructs His children gently. It took many years for my stubborn heart to understand what Jesus meant when He spoke to his disciples in Matthew 11:28-30 "Come to me all who are weary, and I will give you rest. Take my yoke upon you and learn from me, for I am gentle and lowly in heart, and you will find rest for your souls. For my yoke is easy and my burden is light" (Matthew 11:28-30 NLT).

Jesus knows the truth of what will happen if we hold onto our burdens alone: they're too heavy to bear, weighing us down. We become exhausted slaves to bitterness, choking us and suffocating the life and breath God wants to give. When we come to Jesus, we must be ready and willing to admit we are tired and need to breathe. He invites us to surrender, to stop striving, and to release our control. He says to us, "take my yoke, learn from me."

I think everyone on the day they acknowledge their need for Christ should be told: "Now, go learn from Jesus." What do I mean when I say "learn"? I mean be eager to listen, be teachable and moldable, ask for wisdom and be curious. That makes you a disciple growing in your spiritual maturity as you desire to know more of who God is and what His word teaches. It is a wonderful day when we finally surrender and see our need for a Savior, but it is not a day that holds a magic fix to our wounds or struggles. Jesus forgives us and washes them white as snow, but we must continually bring our struggles to the feet of Jesus.

"Learn from me, for I am gentle and lowly in heart." Now tell me, friend, let us get honest here, do we really, truly know this gentle and lowly Jesus? We get the message that Jesus died on the cross. God showed us grace in that while we were still sinners, He sent His son Jesus. We can get the message that we can lay our burdens down, a task that seems easy. But do we really know how to follow through with it?

Many Christians today believe all their sin and brokenness is covered by grace, and it is. It is the wonderful hope we have in the Good News of Jesus. But that is not the whole story. We were not saved from our sin on the cross so we can continue to live how we want and carry around the same bag of garbage. We weren't meant to suffer under the weight of sin our whole lives. Jesus did not hang on the cross and hand out free passes into heaven. He bore the full weight of our sin. He took our punishment. He felt the deep agony of being separated from God the Father as we were separated and cut off before Christ came. Jesus cried out to the Father, "Forgive them for they don't know what they are doing" (Luke 23:34 NLT). We were prideful and arrogant; we hung an innocent man on the cross and then mocked him and tormented him. But He still showed great love and gentleness toward us in his darkest hour of pain and isolation.

Let us learn from Jesus and model our lives after Him. He was gentle and lowly, He loved us while He was hanging on the cross. He was abandoned. We were mocking him and He still loved us at that moment. If you claim to belong to Christ and there are any sins you enjoy holding onto, those sins were nailed to the cross. He crucified them there in that moment when he was abandoned and left to die, so you wouldn't have to be a slave to them anymore. He did that for you so you could be set free, delivered from the burden and protected from enemy attacks.

We were in one of the hives closing their home for the winter season and saw that we never put a divider board in this hive. It was a smaller colony, only filling out half the box. Bees don't like extra space. It is harder for them to guard against intruders. We went through each frame to check for beetles or wax worms and to peek on the queen when I noticed they had completely glued shut their second entrance with thick propolis. It can be applied so thick it grows hard as a rock, and I thought how brilliant these tiny creatures are. God even designed them to protect against enemy attacks and close every crack. They barricade themselves in, especially in preparation for colder months. They really do not need the beekeeper, but we act as guards watching over their colony, cleaning up the excess they cannot keep up with at times or when drone bees (boy bees) start taking over and consuming all their resources. Fall season comes around and those drone bees get kicked out, the girls clean house, and beekeepers are there to keep watch.

The more we get to know Jesus, the more we want to confess the sin in our dark heart and ask Him to help us close those cracks where Satan can sneak into and find a foothold. We want to get rid of the darkness, to throw the garbage out of our lives and barricade our hearts from attacks Satan wants to throw. When we fall in love with the Jesus of the Bible, we start to see God has our best interest in mind. He designed us in His image, for His glory, to worship Him all the days of our lives. That beautiful, perfect design was broken when sin entered the garden, but God sent Jesus to begin the restoration process and give us the tools we need to protect and guard our hearts. We must learn from Jesus and go on the path toward healing and wholeness. It does not disappear the moment we declare that we believe in Him, though. The Lord wants us to walk intimately with Him, getting to know Him by reading His word. As we grow deeper in the knowledge of who He is, we are transformed by the Holy Spirit from the inside out and we become more lovely.

In our early years of marriage, I was walking around a neighborhood garage sale with my husband when I spotted an old tin mug with whimsical flowers and bees buzzing. The words "bee lovely" were written in vintage cursive. For a whole quarter, I took that mug home and used it as a succulent pot. That little tin mug has followed me many miles through many moves, and it has sat on every one of my kitchen window sills since. Every time I would do the monotonous chore of scrubbing dishes, I would look up and see the words "bee lovely." I sure didn't feel lovely. I carried a lot of baggage and shame into my marriage.

I had not learned the lesson of letting go of baggage as a newlywed but finding that lovely tin mug was the first step toward God taking my heart gently into His hands and showing me loveliness. God was calling me back to Himself and speaking to me in small ways. I started noticing little things in the stillness all around me. Even in an antique store, I could sense God speaking to me about my own pain just by gazing at the objects and imagining the stories tied to each piece. I began to hear His voice more clearly as I allowed Him to teach me how He sees me as a woman, a daughter, and a wife. He was writing His story on the pages of my life.

He is so patient with us. Long suffering is a word we cannot understand until we experience how long God waits for us to come to Him. He waits until we are willing to learn, and He is gracious to teach us what our hearts need to grow. We are not the center of the story, He is. And He is changing us little by little. Our blooming process is a life-long lesson, and one day we will see Him and praise Him for it all. We cannot see Him clearly unless our hearts are pure. It is in His goodness of allowing trials that He purifies us. That is what He is doing in our trials. He is refining us and clearing away the clutter, burning away the dross.

Loveliness leaves a sweetness on the lips. Every woman longs to be lovely and to be loved, to discover our soft femininity and blossom as the woman He intended us to be. God originally designed us to be perfect and good, sin entered and that loveliness has been tainted over time. Some of us have been worn down and ragged. A lovely garden can be overcome by aphids eating the plants you so lovingly planted or rodents eating the fruit you so patiently grew, but that does not mean we throw our hands up and toss a pile of dirt on the whole garden.

There is a slinky deceiver, Satan, who is sneaking around that we must acknowledge. He is very clever in his mission to tear down the goodness of God and His superior design. He looks for any entrance, any tiny crack, and he weasels his way into our thoughts to begin planting seeds of doubt. Maybe you feel your wounds are holding you back, your baggage is weighing you down, and the lies in your head have become true. Maybe you're just so broken that you are feeling beyond repair. May as well toss the dirt on the pile and quit, right?

That is not God's way. You are still lovely and that is how God sees you, even if the scheme of Satan seems to be overshadowing the beauty within. God still loves you and He is still there working in the background, faithfully tending to the soil of your heart. Notice the bees in the background going from flower to flower, they don't stop working. God never stops working in your life either. He sees you through Christ who is covering you with His grace. God sees you as perfect.

I carried a piece of baggage long into my marriage that was blocking the sunlight and preventing the loveliness from growing. I loved swimming. My earliest memories surrounded summers at the pool, growing up on the swim team and racing at all the meets. I loved everything about the pool deck. I loved the adrenaline build up to the starting block, the smell of chlorine, and the sounds of the bustling pool deck. But what I loved most was the total silence under the water and the stillness no one could touch. No matter how misunderstood I felt or how loud my thoughts were, I could hide under the water, and it would all be silenced.

Then swim season in my sophomore year of high school, I had a new coach who stole that simple joy from me with an impulse he could not resist. He had a hypnotic control over me, the way his eyes would search for mine the moment he stepped onto the pool deck. It did not matter that I was not attracted to him, but when our eyes locked, my heart would race. I found myself searching for him at every practice and the effect he had on me thickened. He started to touch me in places no man has the right to touch, and I let him. I felt helpless to stop him. I just let his hands wander and explore as my skin was crawling. Inside, I was screaming, but my voice could not find its way to the surface. It left me feeling guilty and shameful in the deepest parts of my soul, like I was sinking to the silent depths of the pool.

I did not feel lovely. I felt ruined like a sunflower sprout lopped off by a deer, never to bloom or feel the warm summer sun on my face. After that day, the water turned to ice, I lost my joy for swimming and I refused to go to practice. I used every excuse not to go. I was so close to achieving my goal of qualifying for state level competition and I just shut down inside. Satan found a crack and I let him in. I locked that memory in a box and buried it far back in a dark room of my heart, never to see the light of day. I did not realize how holding that secret in the dark would influence the choices I would make for the next eight years and the heavy burdens that I would carry into marriage. I never shared that secret with another soul until my husband was pounding down the locked door of the bathroom in our first year of marriage. I was trapped in the darkness of my thoughts, and I couldn't let him in. I could not expose the secret that held me captive or fully grasp the wall hindering our intimacy. The lies were taking over and clouding my mind. There were intimate parts of my heart I could never quite give to my husband, and he was not giving up until that door was down. I was making a tangled mess of my marriage, but God in His goodness took the tangled mess and He continued to work at each knot. He is not just restoring us for our own good, it is for His glory. He uses life circumstances to redeem and restore what was broken if we allow Him.

Sometimes He gives us the right spouse who can see past the pain and is willing to knock down those doors to get to our heart, or a friend who notices we are more than our wounds and will love us unconditionally. It is a process we must choose to humble ourselves, let God soften our hearts and be willing to bring those locked up, hidden boxes out of the back room into the light.

I broke down that day in the bathroom. My husband lovingly took me in his arms, and he just held me as my body was shaking in sobs. The Lord is gentle and lowly. He wraps his arms around us when we break down in surrender and he meets us there. We are already cleansed and purified, but we begin to see that cleansing power through our step of surrender. Cry those hot tears and let Him break down the dam.

My stubborn heart took a long time to be set free in our marriage. I had to be willing to follow the shame to the root cause and identify why I was reacting in such a sinful, self-focused way. It wasn't until I took the opportunity to go to an Awaken Love marriage class that I started to peel back the pain I had brought into marriage and uncover what was hindering intimacy. We can ask for help and the Lord will present opportunities. I grabbed hold of this opportunity and soaked up every bit of wisdom the instructor had to share. My heart softened when I heard other stories that I was not alone. We are more connected and intertwined as sisters in Christ than we realize. We will never be perfect, but God sees us as perfect and beautiful. We may feel complicated and messy, but He sees His daughters as lovely.

I may be able to share a nugget of hope, but I would rather you learn from Jesus. We live in a world where the light seems to be growing dimmer. The darkness seems to be taking over, but really, it is not. If we are spending time in our Bible, we will see what God is weaving behind the scenes. If we know our Bible, the world will make more sense. The darkness may seem to be overshadowing the light right now, but the light is growing brighter right alongside the darkness. The light is more power-ful than the dark. God's word says one day the light will burst forth, the clouds will roll back like a scroll, and Jesus will return. It will be a glorious day. We can turn our eyes to Jesus, we can look to Him and all the things we struggle with fade to the background.

For now, we wait as a woman experiencing birth pangs (Matt. 24:8 NLT), the Bible says. We wrestle and toil, we work out our salvation in fear and trembling (Phil. 2:12 NLT). If we are looking to Jesus, He teaches us to rest and shows us who we were created to be; lovely beings created to worship our Creator.

I was learning to listen to His still small voice speaking to me, "Just *bee* who I made you to be. Be the lovely daughter I made you to be." I was learning to discern the truth from the lies, to recognize and rediscover the truth of who I am in Christ, not the version of myself I had formed by believing lies and making poor life choices. He was restoring me – and continues to restore the broken pieces in me.

We can make a mess of our life, but we are never beyond repair. We can continue to let the mess pile up, make the same choices that lead us into pain, or we can turn back to Jesus and repent. God can completely heal wounds in an instant. That miracle was ours when Jesus went to the cross.

The Bible says we are a new creation (2 Cor. 5:17) and that we are more than conquerors (Rom. 8:37). But sometimes, even as a new creation we can fall into old patterns or find ourselves struggling with sin. There may still be times when we are stubborn to surrender. We can choose daily to give Him a little more and let Him work on our hearts. We can choose to do the hard thing of humbling ourselves and admitting the sin we keep holding onto. The more we are willing to yield to Him and let go, the more we can be cleansed of all unrighteousness. We become like our Teacher and if we are looking to Jesus to teach us, He will mold us into His image.

We can take steps into the light and God meets us there. Maybe you are hesitant to step forward. That's okay. Maybe you have become so accus-tomed to living in the shadows that now you do not feel safe anywhere. If you can find just an ounce of courage to step into the light, you will find Jesus waiting there for you with open arms. You can choose to bring those dusty boxes of painful memories out of the back room of your heart and let the comforting arms of Jesus lighten your load. As He heals your heart bit by bit, your burdens will start to feel lighter, and you will find freedom. As we spend time in the light of Jesus, we start seeing (maybe for the first time) that we are truly lovely, and that God made us to be this way. We were made in His image; to be beekeepers and painters, dancers and singers, mothers, and daughters; for the purpose of living it out and reflecting the glory and mercy of our Lord. He made you, and when He completed His masterpiece, He called you *good*.

What do you see when you look at yourself?

Do you see yourself as lovely?

Search your heart and find the secrets and locked up boxes hidden deep within. Write them down.

What burdens are you carrying? Do they feel too heavy?

**Action step #3.**

Go walk around your local antique store or thrift store (if you love thrifting as much as I do!) and just saunter. If you hate shopping, walk around a flower shop, a library, or a candy shop. The purpose of this step is to look for a lovely little item that makes you smile. Bring it home and set it on your windowsill or hang it on your wall. Many times, in Scripture, the Israelites set up altars to remember God's goodness and faithfulness of what He has done. He will speak to your heart in the way you need that day and show you a token of His goodness. Remember He sees you as good, He thinks you are lovely. I would sure enjoy having coffee with you and getting to know your loveliness.

# WHERE DID THE LORD

*lead you*

## TODAY?

### DID YOU FIND A TOKEN OF HIS GOODNESS?

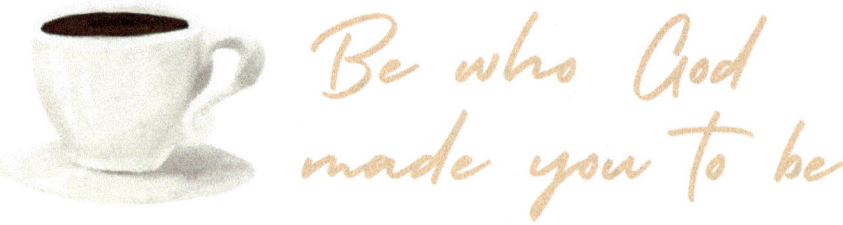
*Be who God made you to be*

"THEREFORE IF ANYONE IS IN CHRIST, HE IS A NEW CREATION. THE OLD HAS PASSED AWAY; BEHOLD THE NEW HAS COME."
2 CORINTHIANS 5:17 ESV

Noticing a bee working in the vibrant goldenrod as I'm working side by side with my best friend reset my perspective and set my mind on what truly matters. God designed us to do what we love and bring Him glory.

# chapter 4

A seed has to be planted and die before it can sprout. The process can be painful, but the fruit that comes is well worth it. Locking myself behind the bathroom door was a stronghold that took root long before entering marriage, and confronting it took me back into the pits of darkness. When I was a young teenager, I was experiencing suicidal thoughts, the opposite of what I was witnessing at church. I was trapped in the dark prison of my own head. I was believing God did not care, He did not notice me. Notice is a word that, unknown to me at the time, would cause a lot of knots in my life, ones I wouldn't recognize until 20 years later when I started to see that trail of sin in my own children. When we follow the lie to its roots, it will lead to a point in our history or past generations. That is when we can acknowledge the lie and bring it into the light. We can choose to take a step of faith and confess it and that's where Jesus meets us in our obedience. As a young girl I went up to the altars for prayer week after week and the pastor was "chipping away at the iceberg," he called it. He was persistently praying for me. He consistently cared about me in my dark season and prayed fervently.

I knew somewhere in my heart these issues were a generational pattern and I wanted to be freed from the heavy, dark cloud weighing over me. The suicidal thoughts were dark, and many nights I woke up scared of the demons I was seeing. Some would toss it off as night terrors and go on with life, but it was a real battle in my bedroom. I would lock myself in the bathroom to get away from the scary world outside, but behind those doors the dark thoughts had power over me. I would use scissors to slice my skin and get the pain I was feeling inside to pour out. All I could hear repeatedly was, "no one notices, no one cares, just end it." I came from a church going family with praying parents and yet the lies "no one notices or cares" had a stronghold on my mind. I believed I was unimportant and invisible. No one noticed the torment I was wrestling with inside and I was continually seeking validation. I appeared to be a confident, happy young girl but inside I was silently suffering.

One night, that pastor came to my house and broke the bathroom door down. He kept faithfully caring for me and chipping away at the block. I will never forget the day, one Sunday night at an altar-call, that "block" broke. We both felt it and just started praising the Lord. We raised our hands up and thanked God for breaking the oppression over me. I did not pick up another sharp object again until my first year of marriage when Satan dangled that same torment over my mind. He used the same tactic for a different purpose. That depression had no hold on me any longer, but Satan still used the word "notice" to continue knotting me up in other ways and seducing me away from Christ.

All my life I tried to muster up more of the fruit of joy. "Be joy like your middle name" my mom would say, but we cannot force ourselves to be more joyful with self-help and mantras. Even when the Bible says in Philippians 4:4 (NLT), "Always be full of joy in the Lord. I say it again – Rejoice!" The key words are to be joyful in the Lord. He is where we find our joy. Rejoicing in Him is a choice of obedience. When we obey what the Lord is asking, we will be filled with joy. Fruit comes from obedience. By nature, we run away from obedience, plug our ears, and pretend we did not hear anything.

Running starts when we are old enough to take our first steps. Mommy says to come, and we run in the opposite direction. Toddlers think it is a fun game of chase and giggle all the way out the door. As we grow, we begin to learn obedience actually matters for a bigger reason than we could understand.

I was standing on the end of a boat launch dock one evening and the wind was whipping. I was in awe of our Creator who controls the wind and the waves. When I turned to the left, the wind was loud in my ear. I faced forward again, and it was quiet. Then, turning to the right, the wind was loud. You get the idea, but it was apparent the Lord speaks to us in the wind and He speaks in the stillness when we look forward.

When we turn to the right or to the left, we can begin to veer off path and get distracted by the louder voices of the world. We can wonder why the load feels so heavy or how the weight of the world is piled on our shoulders. When we face forward in focus to hear from God, He will be faithful to lead. The truth of today is we have many distractions on many sides and deceptions fighting for our attention. We must fight for that focus, to stay walking forward with the Lord.

In our formative years, we unknowingly get caught up in those deceptions. Some can be damaging while others can be very subtle, and we can go years before realizing we believed them. Let's follow this thread for a bit and unravel some of these lies. Satan is the father of lies and we must be willing to follow the knots to find freedom. Satan's number one goal is to get you to doubt God and not trust His plan. He enjoys tying up knots in your life and distracting you. He takes immense pleasure in seducing you off course.

I grew up in a church that taught Jesus loves me and died for me, but the core of the gospel did not make it into the inner chambers of my heart. I did not understand that obedience is where I find the missing puzzle piece of joy. Jesus said in Matthew 16 (NLT), "If any of you wants to be my follower, you must give up your own way, take up your cross and follow me." I did not understand that turning from my selfish ways was a conscious choice to walk forward in obedience. Although I grew up in a healthy, thriving church in an era when people were excited to attend church, it did not shield me from lies or misconceptions. People were alive and free in Christ and were being filled with the baptism of the Holy Spirit in large numbers. It was a revival era. I watched many go up to the altars for prayer and leave praising and dancing. They were finding freedom and joy by stepping forward in obedience to go to Jesus and laying down their burdens. I looked forward to going to church every time the doors were open. I witnessed miracles and healings. I watched people walk in their giftings and talents, praising the Lord with their whole heart, voices singing out and hands lifted high. It really was a joyful place to be and many times what felt like a glimpse of heaven. We would spend hours in the presence of the Lord and pray at the altars. I had genuine encounters with the Lord that no one can take away. I was completely healed and freed from certain generational patterns.

We cannot muster up this kind of inner bubbling joy in our own strength or muster up enough willpower to live joyful lives. Sometimes obedience requires an action step, and any action requires faith, even if it is only the size of a mustard seed. We find joy in that forward motion. I have found the path forward is the path of peace. The Lord isn't going to lead us off course or distract us in the noise on our right or left. We are to put on the shoes of peace, it says in Ephesians 6. He is a God of peace and if we are listening to Him in the stillness, He will be faithful to lead the way.

I am not naive to the fact that my home church growing up had its imperfections and flaws, but the presence of the Lord was there. It was undeniable. People were laying their burdens down at the cross and walking away full of joy they could not contain. It was not just a nice 3-point sermon. Our pastor didn't just preach a simple message, then send us back home bearing the same burdens. We were led to the cross, to the altars, to lay down our burdens. We were taught how to pray. We were taught how to do the challenging work of stepping out and pressing forward. Sometimes it takes an action step. We can listen to sermons every day and read all the theology books in the world, but if there is no action step of faith forward, it means nothing – it is dead. "Faith without good deeds is dead" (James 2:17 NLT). We must hear what we are taught and let the Holy Spirit compel us toward transformation. In that process of surrender and humility, hearts were being tightly knit together and lifelong bonds were being formed. We were a family, brothers and sisters in Christ. Of course we still had struggles but we loved each other deeply.

Then, something I never expected to see happened. The church family was being attacked. I watched the slow crumble of the Church happen over a span of fifteen years. Satan attacks all the good God designed: marriage, family, and the church body. I watched as prayer meetings were being taken off the weekly schedule and replaced with watching the nightly news at home, fellowship halls became coffee shops, and instead of empty hands and humble hearts ready to worship, people started bringing their coffees into service. I watched the fear of the Lord being drowned out in the cacophony of friendly chatter. The power of God was disregarded. People lost sight of the reverence and awe of who God is and they were growing increasingly complacent. They lost sight of the Mighty works He could do, and they allowed doubt to infiltrate their hearts. It became a place of casual worship and routine. The Church was messy and full of sinful, broken people and it is still messy today. I love the Church, but the brokenness can inflict some deep cuts to our faith and cause profound questioning.

If we look at Church history, we see it has been a slow crumbling since the beginning, but we also see it has had its times of revivals and reformations. There were always pockets of people fighting to keep the core roots alive. Satan has been working to squelch God's good plan for the Church. But God has also had a plan for His people since the beginning, a plan to restore and revive, and His plan is the one that will prevail.

We learn from scripture to "Fix our thoughts on what is true, honorable, right, pure, lovely, and admirable." We think about these things that are excellent and worthy of praise, but Paul goes on to say, "Keep putting into practice all you learned and received from me—everything you heard from me and saw me doing. Then the God of peace will be with you" (Phil. 4:9 NLT). At church growing up, I watched this being put to practice. I watched people get healed miraculously because there was an environment that allowed for miracles to happen. People were not chained up in fear, sin, and shame. They were bringing their struggles into the light; they were confessing their sin, and they were turning away from their shame. The Lord was meeting them in their darkest hour and leading them into marvelous light. It required a step of obedience. It required a willingness to look weird, but in the end they were free. It did not matter how they looked to others. It did not matter what others thought of them. There is an element of faith to get past our logic and see the glimmer of light at the end. Faith defies logic. Obedience steps out when logic says stay silent.

In Christ, we are created new as it says in Ephesians 2. He sets our feet on a new path, and we do not have to go back to the darkness. We don't have to share that secret or lay that burden down and then take it back. It is at the feet of Jesus. He takes it. He delivers you from it. Like a prisoner living in exile for years, you are liberated. Once you taste that bubbling over, abundant freedom and joy, you don't want to go back. Why would you want to? How could you? After experiencing a glimpse of heaven after being in such torment. I was finding freedom but watching my church crumble sent me into a spiral of deep questioning, one that did not bring me to a revelation of the true gospel right away.

I was trying to find a way in my own strength and logic to obey instead of being obedient when God opened a door. Sometimes we are asked to do something specific and the swirling in our soul can't be tamed until we obey. Other times, the Lord says to be still and wait. For many years I lived in the tension that if I speak boldly then I'm too intense and if I do not speak honestly then I am not saying enough. I was trying to obey but it was never enough. All I seemed to do was ruffle feathers and could never obey in the right ways. I am still tempted to fall into this trap of bondage but when I go to the quiet place with the Lord and tune out the "too much, not enough" voices, I can hear the task and purpose He has prepared for me long ago in Christ Jesus (Ephesians 2:10 NLT).

Obedience is the task and purpose. Obedience follows the Shepherd's quiet voice. We must be quiet to hear what He is asking us to do. I wonder, do we slow down and ask? We would sing the hymn "Be Still, My Soul" at Grandma's church "Be still my soul the Lord is on thy side, Bear patiently the cross of grief or pain Leave to thy God to order and provide In every change, He faithful will remain Be still, my soul, thy best, thy heavenly friend Through thorny ways leads to a joyful end." I know the deep pit of despair and pain. I did not understand as a young girl why this great God seemed to let me suffer in silence. I was going to church and had parents who loved the Lord, so the darkness that would surround me or the screaming thoughts that would torment me didn't make sense. It was God's mercy and caring people who discipled me that led me out of the darkness into the marvelous light. I never wanted to return. That does not mean Satan stopped his schemes. He doesn't relent once we claim our faith in Jesus. But after that day at the altar, my feet were set on a new path of faith. I was freed from the bondage of living in the darkness. The chain was broken, and my children would not get that link passed down to them.

God did the mighty work of sacrificing His own son Jesus so we would not have to live in that darkness any longer. He made a way for us to break the chains and walk in freedom. Before that bondage of sin existed, we were walking wild and free. Adam and Eve were walking naked and wildly unashamed in the garden, intimately by the Lord's side. We were meant to walk intimately with God until Satan's schemes worked and he seduced them away from the Lord. They took a bite of the forbidden fruit. We are still being seduced away from the Lord everyday, whether we realize it or not. We must know our Enemy's tactics and schemes to know how to fight back or stand against. His goal is to trip us up or distract us to the right or left but God's voice is straightforward in the quiet. We carry the choice to continue being tripped, or even fall down day after day, allowing Satan to hold the power over us, or we can walk in obedience to what God's word is leading us to do.

Daniel stayed faithful to the path God set his feet on. He and his people were living in exile, in a land that was not their home. He was deeply rooted in his faith, serving God with all his heart, faithfully following the Lord, and obeying each step over his whole lifetime. While he was living under the authority of a king who did not fear the Lord, the king signed a decree stating that no one could pray to any other god. Instead, they must bow down to him. Daniel continued obeying God in prayer as he always had. He did not change his daily life or crumble under compliance when the king put out a new law. Daniel feared God and obeyed what He was

62

leading him to do each day, even if that meant a night spent with hungry lions. We listen to God and obey Him first above any other.

Daniel did not go looking for ways to obey God or please Him. He was obeying and pleasing God with his faithful, daily living. When the opportunity arose to deny God or give in to man, he stayed true to the path he was already walking. God protected him and Daniel trusted God even if it meant losing his life. He was still on the path with God either way.

Joy comes from our obedience to God no matter what He is asking us to do. If we know and we are certain of what He is asking, we will be focused and fulfilled in walking that out. In scripture, James talks about coming to the Lord with faith and we will not be so easily tossed by the wind. Timothy talks about the importance of recognizing we don't have a spirit of fear, but we are to have a sound mind (2 Tim.1:7 NLT). When our identity is in Christ and our faith grows deeper with him, we won't comply so easily with what others are doing. We will not be so easily pulled into the pit of second guessing ourselves when we are strong in the Lord and confident in where He is leading us. We can come boldly to the throne of God's grace like Daniel did three times a day and know we are exactly where God wants us. When we learn the gospel and decide to put our trust in Jesus, we give Him our whole life, our whole heart. We begin to pray, "Not my will Lord but Your will be done," as Jesus taught his disciples how to pray in Matthew 6:9-13 (NLT). We begin to fully grasp what Jesus really did on the cross and we want to give Him our life. We want to obey what He is asking us to do because we recognize the sacrifice He made on the cross for us. Like Jesus telling his disciples to turn from their selfish ways and pick up their cross to follow Him, we are to deny ourselves, turn away from our selfishness, and listen to what He is asking us to do. That message of sacrificial living did not make it to my heart for a long time. I wanted to do something important for God in some far-off land instead of obeying what He was asking me to do right here in my present day, and that lesson would take me on a bumpy road across the country and through many churches before I could begin to see the truth clearly.

What task has God put on your heart that you're putting off?

How can you throw off the heaviness holding you down today?

What is one way you can walk in obedience to the Lord today?

**Action step #4.**

You can sit still and keep that seat warm, or you can follow that still quiet voice nudging you to take a step with that "box" you have kept in hiding. There is someone you need to forgive or a lie plaguing your mind. Go to a peaceful place in nature and write what comes to mind in your Notice Notebook. Then just listen to what the Lord is leading you to do with that "box." He wants you to be strong and courageous, and bring that box out into the light. If your church has a prayer time, take a step, and ask for prayer. If it's your spouse you need to talk to, or you have a trusted friend, admit you are struggling and need help. If it is a deeper nagging struggle, you can find freedom with a God-fearing Christian counselor who can help unpack the box. If you aren't sure where to start in prayer, go to your knees and write out Matthew 6:9-13. We have never met but we are sisters in Christ and I am praying for you right now.

*Lord, I ask you to gently guide my sister to peaceful waters, restore her soul and lead her in the way she should go. Let your will be done on earth as it is in heaven. Give her daily bread and help her forgive. Lead her not into temptation but deliver her from the evil one. Show her how You see her today and bring her a token of your love. In Your name I ask. Amen.*

# *Obedience*
# PRODUCES FRUIT

"OUR FATHER IN HEAVEN HALLOWED BE YOUR NAME, YOUR KINGDOM COME, YOUR WILL BE DONE, ON EARTH AS IT IS IN HEAVEN." MATTHEW 6:9-10

PRAY HIS WILL BE DONE.
THEN ASK WHAT IS ONE STEP OF
OBEDIENCE YOU CAN DO?

# BEE HUMBLE
## chapter 5

Even when we choose the narrow path of obedience, we are going to be humbled. We went on a humbling journey in our first decade of marriage through many churches, and when I say many, I mean more than thirty. We were involved and committed to six during that time, trying our best to genuinely connect and serve in our area of gifting. I came into marriage with my Christian ministry degree, we both had much experience in missions work and traveling the world, and we were eager to know the big plans God was going to unfold. We were ready to go anywhere, but it didn't take long to see that our young ideals did not fit the mold of the institutional Church. We were not allowed to step into any role or speak in any capacity when the Holy Spirit led us to. We were members at one church, committed to a year-long leadership training. When Sam approached the pastor with feedback and different visions for starting ministries that were needed within that church family, his response was for us to respect his leadership and follow his vision for the church or we were welcome to leave. He left us with no other option but to walk away. There was no freedom for the Spirit to move or room for new sprouts to grow. We were backed up against a wall like a flower trying to grow within four walls of a cardboard box. I was looking to the church to satisfy my longing for purpose and to know more of God but we kept running up against the same wall at every turn, wondering why nothing was working, and circling back to the humbling lesson in Proverbs 16:9 (NLT): "We can make our plans, but God determines our steps." We don't set out on a path anticipating a dead end, nor do we know what is up ahead. We make our plans and try to stay faithful, but God orders our steps and changes our direction. He was gently leading us onto a new path outside the walls of the church.

We had seasons of lulls between churches when we were not members anywhere, and we would try attending a few others but all we saw was the same disheartening reality. We could walk into some churches and see as an outsider with fresh eyes all the red flags and cracks in the foundation. There was one year we decided to do an intentional "church tour" and visit a different church every week. We felt this compelling from the Holy Spirit to get a better grasp on the true condition of the Church as a whole and get a broader picture of God's heart for His Church. We visited thirteen churches, and we started recognizing the same patterns. Pastors were using the same language, referring to the same books or idolizing the same authors. Did they all get fed the same information from the same conference? I had to wonder. There was a model we were seeing that felt forced and rehearsed—a model being implemented that seemed like religion glued together with routine.

Many churches had become starch and stale, seeming to be stuck on doctrine and theology without knowledge of the Spirit's leading. It is crucial to read God's Word for ourselves and evaluate the fruit of leaders. They are not always aligned with God's word and led by the Holy Spirit. Ministry degrees and pastoral titles are not what qualify a person to lead a flock in Godly ways. I spent six years in ministry school and know how easy it can be to fall into the trap of merely regurgitating head knowledge for the test.

It was apparent the needs of God's people were not being met and spiritual depravity was evident. There was no life, no breath, no joy. Each church was lacking, and we could see the missing piece: the Holy Spirit. We could still sense His presence in some of the people, but the Spirit of the Lord was fading to the background. The people didn't even realize He was fading or know the gift they were missing. When I would look out into the crowd, I would see the same stark sadness in people's eyes. Very rarely did I see anyone raising their hands or praising the Lord. I found an emptiness that went much deeper than any ritualized Sunday service could fix, and I would sit there wondering if they had prayer meetings, Bible study groups, or any safe place to find healing and freedom.

I would look at their church bulletin in my hands and see very few opportunities on the schedule for gathering and nurturing those church family bonds. It hurt my heart to see another beautiful church building sitting empty all week while their members went home suffering with the same sadness week after week. It was cold and disconnected. They could join a community group, but that was often the only option. I'm sure there are some wonderful community groups around, but again, in our experience, we only found the disconnected, counterfeit version of what the Bible teaches true community to be- a picture of joy and eagerness to be around other brothers and sisters in Christ. I knew there was so much more missing and I longed for more. The Holy Spirit is full of life and breath, He nurtures a sense of community that displays a rich love for each other. The Bible talks about greeting each other with a sacred kiss (2 Cor. 13:12 NLT) when Paul closes his letter with "brothers and sisters," and we could not find evidence of the Holy Spirit, that phileo love, or deep brotherly love, anywhere within the institution.

We saw the slow crumble, as if watching a mold gradually melt, and there was nothing we could do to stop it. We faced the same decision every time we went to a new church—commit to the mess and allow God to use us however He willed, or continue searching. There would be signs of humility and desire for growth in the churches where we felt led to stay at but as our relationships grew closer, it became more evident the heart of the church was not pursuing deeper intimacy with the Lord. The heart of Jesus is to never forget our first love. It was never received well when we brought attention to an area needing growth. We were willing to step into the need, but we were told it was the staff's job and we could sign up for one of the volunteer roles. I looked at the options of boxes to check and never fit any of them.

Jesus never trained his disciples to be volunteers, and he didn't need to train them to obey. They simply walked with Him side by side, and they learned obedience as they spent time with Jesus. It was a more natural camaraderie of friendship, and their faith deepened without even realizing it. We were trying to fit into the mold established by church leaders and it felt forced, rigid, and routine. It was the opposite of a living, breathing organism. We were searching for a church where the body of Christ was thriving, and every time we found our courage to step out, we were faced with disappointment yet again. It humbled us further with each new season we found ourselves having church time at home, not knowing how we could connect to the local church that seemed lifeless.

Time and again, we had no choice but to step away from the institutional church, and the temptation to hide in my cage of familiar self-pity and loneliness would rear up again. Those seasons of loneliness started to become less about self and more about discovering this deeper intimacy with God. My heart was being humbled and softened, changing into the likeness of Christ, and a completely unexpected thing of beauty was beginning to sprout. I was finding freedom in Christ, freedom to be who He made me to be and live in the ways He gifted me.

I found that true freedom in Christ was not attached to a denomination or a church building; it wasn't attached to a theology or doctrine. It wasn't even attached to my ministry degree I had worked so hard to achieve. That piece of paper turned out to be just a piece of paper. It did not define my worth if a pastor noticed my ability to step into a role or not. A pastor shouldn't hold the power if we are capable of ministering anyway. We answer to God, not man, and man doesn't dictate what we are called to do. I often ended up doing nothing and went through my days aimlessly without vision because the pastor had squelched my calling. God's Word says we are to respect authority as Romans 13:1-7 (NLT) teaches, but it doesn't say to be a compliant sheep to that voice of authority.

This may be uncomfortable to hear, but it may not be to follow the vision of a pastor at all. The Bible says "Where there is no vision the people perish, but he that keepeth the law happy is he" (Prov. 29:18 KJV) or another way to hear it "When people do not accept divine guidance, they run wild, but whoever obeys the law is joyful" (Prov. 29:18 NLT). We follow God's revelation not what a man tells us his vision is for us to follow. God may lead you to commit to a church family and really love them well, but He may lead you outside the walls on a completely different path than you think. We will be aimless or run wild without vision until we follow God's divine guidance. When we love His law and obey His leading we find freedom. Pastors have their place, but God also needs missionaries to go across the globe, evangelists to stoke the fire, teachers to passionately plant the truth of God's Word into hearts, prophets to tune into His voice, and apostles to challenge Christ-followers to a deeper faith. We can easily fall into the deception of following a pastor simply because he was put in a position of authority, but he may be leading his sheep astray. If we are diligently seeking God with our whole heart, reading His Word for ourselves, and listening to His still quiet voice, He is going to show us which way to go like the Good Shepherd leads His sheep. We can respect a pastor, but God could be leading us to go in a completely different direction than the vision of that pastor, and it is our responsibility to follow those promptings for ourselves. We don't have to force ourselves to fit into a box if we are growing in depth of intimacy with God and He is leading us another way. It may feel safer to stay where it is comfortable but sometimes Jesus asks us to have faith and step out, like Peter in the storm. Peter said, "Lord if it's really you, tell me to come to you, walking on the water" (Matt.14:28

NLT). Jesus said "Yes, come." Christ followers will be asked to do the uncomfortable at times, to go out into unfamiliar territory and start something completely new. There are still people who need to hear the hope of Jesus and how will they know unless we tell them? How can we tell them unless we get out of our comfortable seats?

For so many years, I was aimlessly walking my own path, following the Church vision of a pastor and listening to the pastoral authority over me, but I was not paying attention to the voice of the Good Shepherd leading me in the way I should go. I was a regular American young adult who drove around in a yellow Volkswagen Beetle with a good job, and I could buy anything I wanted at any time. I was sipping my Starbucks and shopping for clothes, but even in that season, the Good Shepherd was calling my name. I didn't see how spoiled or entitled I was until I started traveling the world and seeing humanity for what it really is. Somewhere deep down even back then, I knew being a Christ-follower meant being set apart, but I was too comfortable to grasp the cost and sacrifice. It felt safe going along with the direction of the church leaders and too unfamiliar to step outside of that path. I didn't understand what sins were lurking or strongholds were taking root that God was going to reveal. I wasn't walking on the road to Damascus on a vengeance to kill Christians like Paul when God stopped me in my tracks and got my attention. It was a slow, gentle, humbling process.

There was a man, Saul, in the Bible who took immense pleasure in holding the power over any Jew who was a Christ-follower. It was his mission to imprison and persecute Christians. He went door to door dragging men and women out to imprison them, his fury growing by the day. When Stephen was so bold to call out and correct the council, their hard hearts only grew harder. They covered their ears, not wanting to hear the truth. Then they dragged Stephen outside to stone him. This day was a turning point for Christ-followers. Saul could have stopped the stoning, instead he watched as they stoned Stephen and did not seem to flinch. He held the power to stop it, but he didn't. It only fueled his fury more and sent him on a rampage to gather all those who believed in Jesus. Saul was living in the darkness of his ways, not wanting to believe Jesus was the Way.

He was on his mission to gather and imprison believers on the road to Damascus when a light from heaven suddenly shone down on him. He fell to the ground and heard a voice saying to him, "Saul! Saul! Why are you persecuting me?" (Acts 9:1-9 NLT). Jesus was speaking to him and showed great mercy on him that day. When he stood up with instructions to continue to Damascus, he was blind. His companions had to lead him the rest of the way, and when they arrived, Saul couldn't see and didn't eat for three days. It wasn't until a man named Ananias was sent by God to lay hands on Saul to let him regain his sight. It wasn't an easy conversion. The Lord showed him how much he would suffer for His name's sake. Ananias, being a Christian, could've feared for his life, but was obedient despite what he had heard about Saul's great hatred for believers in Jerusalem.

When reading the full story of the darkness Saul came from to his conversion and later being commissioned by the Holy Spirit to go preach the good news, the Lord changed his name from Saul to Paul. He was on the road to Damascus for his own purposes, but the Lord set him on a new path that day and changed him from the inside out, completely transforming his heart to then pursue the Lord's purpose for his life. He began his mission to take the message to the Gentiles and to the kings, as well as to Israel.

All I can see in this story is the deep, utter humility he must have felt for God to choose him as His instrument; of all the people God could have chosen, He chose Paul. He chose a man who hated God's people, He chose a man with a heart of stone, and He humbled him that day.

Paul knew how far away and separated from God he was. He knew the darkness he came from and the blindness in his heart. He went from killing God's people for believing Jesus was the Messiah to preaching that Jesus really was the Messiah. Christ-followers feared for their lives, and now Paul was risking his life, preaching the very truth that he killed for. And God simply chose him. He came to him in a great light, took his sight for three days, and restored it back to him. It was pure mercy that God showed Paul to stop him in his tracks and turn him on a new path. Paul knew in that conversion what his mission was. God was directing him to go from town to town, starting with Seleucia as they were sent out by twos. He was awoken from his stupor, brought out of his darkness, shaken from his blindness, and set on a new path with a clear mission to go share the Good News that Jesus really was the Messiah. It was not just for certain people—it was for everyone, Jews and Gentiles.

In the book of Ephesians, Paul preaches to the people of Ephesus the message that we were once all dead because of our disobedience and sin. We all lived in darkness, obeying the devil. He understood the darkness, the hard hearts and deaf ears. He understood the Spirit at work in those hearts who refuse to obey God (Eph. 2:2 NLT). We were all living far away from God, separated from Him and subject to His anger. God could have struck Paul dead on the road to Damascus, but instead he showed mercy, revived his dead heart, and gave him new eyes – both physically regaining sight and spiritual eyes to see truth. Paul did not go on to live comfortably in Damascus and raise a family. That is also a valuable calling to God, but God had a specific mission for Paul. He needed him to be alert and focused without distractions. Imagine being Paul, the person who received insight into God's mysterious plan and purpose through Jesus Christ and to be the one told to go share that news.

That mystery had never been revealed since the beginning, and now God was revealing it to Paul, the man who hadn't believed in Jesus, the man who had killed anyone who did. And God still called Paul His chosen instrument.

Imagine the humility Paul must have felt, the awe and wonder that God showed such great mercy on him. He was dead, and God simply chose to revive him; he was blind, and God gave him sight; he had blinders up to spiritual truth and God removed the veil. Paul had a focused intensity for his purpose in a way many of us can't fully grasp.

If we turn around and look back on all the stepping stones laid out on the ground from the time we were born walking through childhood and teenage years into adulthood, God will reveal that He was faithful every step of the way. He was there at every point and every twist in the road. He was gently calling us by name to come to Him. I can look back and see He was wooing me with such patient mercy, just waiting for me to see the simple truth that He was telling me all along. Paul knew his mission each day, he knew his vision from God and he didn't delay. Paul accepted the vision, God's divine guidance for him and he was joyful in obedience. All along God had a mysterious purpose to sacrifice His son so we could be united with Christ and be brought near to Him through his blood (Eph.2:13 NLT). God revealed this mystery to Paul.

We have to slow down long enough, be still long enough to see the truth revealed with spiritual eyes. God desires for us to learn from Jesus, to be discipled by Him. He was sent to earth to show us the way to the truth. He is the way, He is the truth, He is the life, and no one can come to the Father except through Jesus (John 14:6 NLT). God was tenderly, quietly waiting for me to see that all along I was meant to learn from Jesus. God, in His great ardor, His passionate love for us, a kind of love so deep it hurts, so wide, so vast as the ocean, has been patiently waiting for us to see. He waits for us to see His love. He waits for us to see our need for Jesus.

Jesus modeled everything in his thirty-three years of life that we need to know and follow. His disciples understood and were willing to drop everything, deny themselves, and go with Jesus everyday all day and follow him. They were willing to leave behind families, wives, jobs, and security all because they understood who Jesus was and they wanted to learn from him.

When we see the truth, the truth will set us free, and as Jesus says in the gospel of Matthew, we are to then go and learn. He was saying that once we realize our need for a Savior, that we are sick and in need of a doctor, He tells the people to go forward and learn how to be merciful to others the same way he has shown them mercy. Jesus taught that we are all in need of a Savior but not everyone will have ears to hear. Some will have hardened hearts, unwilling to hear the truth or admit their need for a Savior, but the truth is the same that it's for all people, Jew and Gentile. Jesus came to save all people.

Paul could see the truth with the eyes of his heart when he put his faith in Jesus. He could see how great and how vast the love God the Father showed him, and he saw his purpose that was set out for him long before he knew God had a purpose for him. He saw the purpose in the here and now. He saw his purpose was to obey the Father every day and go where He sent him.

I spent many years believing God had a purpose for me, but it was for "one day," and I kept putting it off. One day, after I get my college degree or meet my pastor husband, then God will show me my mission and we will go and conquer. We will do a great work for God when He reveals to me what that purpose is. It was always for one day and not for today. I was severely twisted up on my theology. The purpose God is talking about that He planned for us in advance was to see our need for Jesus and go share the gospel today, not "one day." He was saying "You know the truth, now go walk in your purpose of sharing that with others so all could know the mercy of God the way you know it." The truth is that we were all living in a cave of darkness, separate from God, and then He reached down His hand to lift us into the marvelous light.

My chain of depression, suicide ideation, and darkness may have been broken at the age of fourteen, but that doesn't mean Satan has stopped trying to pull me back to my dark cave. It's familiar there. It is easy to go back to the familiar, but when we fully experience the marvelous light, we never want to go back again and return to our old pit of despair. We begin to recognize Satan's voice when he is taunting us or tempting us to go back. The baptism of the Holy Spirit gives us the ability to recognize Satan's voice for what it really is and allows us to hear God's voice more clearly. Jesus left us a Helper in the Holy Spirit, and we can turn to Him for guidance when the world tips upside down. He will tell you the truth and separate the truth from the lies. You will start to see with new eyes, spiritual eyes, where you're enabled to discern what is really happening to avoid the same pitfalls. The Israelites went back to their old ways repeatedly, and time and again, God drew them back to Himself. He lifted us out of the darkness every time and placed our feet back on solid ground again. It is in our nature to fall off course back into sinful habits, but when we slow down and come boldly into the presence of God, we can see the beauty was in the honey all along. His still, quiet voice was there in the background just like the constant faithful work of the buzzing bees always there in the background. We just have to slow down long enough to notice the beauty. We must eliminate distractions to see the direction. In a season of pruning and humbling, our faith was about to be tested.

Is your heart soft and open to the Lord?

What areas of your heart do you want Him to come in and do the work of cleaning up?

Are you willing to be humbled even if it's painful?

**Action step #5.**

Get a garbage bag and pick a room in your house. Want me to pull on some gloves and come help? It's time to eliminate some distractions and declutter your mind. Fill one bag, or two, or ten. Maybe you already do this on a regular basis. The action of removing what distracts us sets our feet on a new path and gives our mind room to think and listen. Music can be a help or a hindrance (depends on my mood of the day!) or talking it out with a friend. This may be a step you need to do with just you and God. Get to work, girl!! The reward is worth it, or there's always the secret stash of snacks in the closet (wink!).

# HUMBLE

# HEART

PUT ON THE SONG
"OPEN THE EYES OF MY HEART"
AND SPEND TIME WORSHIPPING.

OUR HEAVENLY FATHER IS WORTHY OF PRAISE.

READ PSALM 19 OUT LOUD

Our bee yard with four Layens hive boxes. They are all raised up higher to stay above tide levels and deter intruders.

# chapter 6

There may be thorns all around, but there is still beauty to be found. If we're willing to look to Jesus and trust Him through those thorny seasons, God will surprise us with gifts along the way and heal us in ways we can't imagine. I can't emphasize this enough. God does amazing work when we choose obedience and stay faithful to the work He is doing in and through us. We can look back and be amazed how the Lord really was working and see how much we grew. We all have a perpetual sin or a struggle that can seem never-ending, but we have the choice to receive the gift of healing in faith and be moldable as God works in our hearts.

There was one season in our marriage when my husband, Sam, slipped into old patterns and was struggling with the sin of pornography. It was a nagging frustration for him, and it was sickening to me. It was causing a slow, drifting wedge between us. I never condemned him or held it against him, and even though we were newly married, it was becoming old news.

Our first baby was born in the coldest winter in decades. Sam was out of work more days than we could afford to be, bills were piling up, and continuing to pay off college debt seemed an impossibility. I was home with our son and not working either. The fear and insecurity started to set in. Sam started talking to me about fasting, and I watched him dive deep into what God's word said about it. We were never taught this in the churches we grew up in. We knew of people who would fast, and our parents would fast occasionally, but we didn't fully grasp the depth or power behind fasting.

The Bible refers to fasting more than seventy times. We were in awe. How had we missed this? But the more we dove in and the deeper we studied, we realized why the Enemy was strategizing and working so hard to hide this tool from believers.

My husband was reading books and talking to anyone who would listen. When he sets his mind on something, he talks about it until he is ready to act. The Lord was leading him to a three-day total fast that would go into twenty-one-day Daniel fast. I watched him transform before my eyes. He was working in freezing conditions (when there was work) on only water, flavorless rice, and saltless vegetables.

He was desperate. He was angry he didn't know about a tool that would help him conquer his perpetual sin cycle. He had some big prayer requests on his list that year, breaking free of pornography addiction being the main one, and I laughed aloud when he told me another – didn't Sarah laugh when God said she would conceive a child at ninety years old? This prayer he shared seemed about as impossible as getting pregnant at ninety. He said God was prompting his heart to be debt-free in one year. I laughed.

He was telling me this as we were sitting at home together, once again not able to go to work in below-zero conditions, wind chill at bone-freezing temperatures. We were staring out at our gloomy apartment courtyard feeling trapped to ever get out of the cycle. I thought he was nuts, it seemed beyond impossible considering our circumstances and my unbelief was stronger than my faith.

But he pressed on and fought his way through the fast, never complaining, never acting like it was taking any of his strength, and I watched him become a different man that year. I sit here writing to you over a decade later, and he never struggled with pornography again. The chain of bondage was broken in that commitment to fasting and prayer. He was completely set free from the addiction. He had two slip-ups, straying into temptation that he quickly confessed, but the Lord changed his heart, and it lost its appeal. The sin lost its power over him and the temptation no longer controlled his mind. As his wife and helper, I check in and he has no desire to stray even a little bit. I am amazed to look back and see the gifts God gave him along the way and the healing that took place in his heart. I watched him go from a place of struggling and suffering to becoming a humbled man, more sensitive to hearing where the Lord was leading him. He was truly repentant and willing to do whatever was asked of him to break free. If we have sin in our heart, it is impossible to hear from God and He won't hear our prayers. Sin cuts us off from God (Isaiah 59:2 NLT). We can confess it and be set free.

That was the first fast we did in our marriage; I didn't join him in the full fast, but it was not going to be our last. We saw the mighty hand of God move on us that year in more ways than I can describe. We had groceries anonymously dropped off at our doorstep, unexpected checks arrived in the mail, doors opened that felt jammed shut for years, and the biggest miracle—within the year, we paid our last college loan check. On one small income with very sparse days of work, we were able to pay off a little more than twenty-five thousand dollars. Only God can do that! We continued to faithfully give money to those in need or tithe throughout the year even when bills were exceeding income. It didn't make logical sense to set aside finances in those ways, but faith defies logic.

Because we obeyed in those small acts of faith, we were able to see the abundant fruit that grew out of that very painful pruning season. God was cutting off the dead branches of unbelief in my heart. There were many days I clung to my husband's steadfast faithfulness, but I sure was being humbled in the process.

The days were long and lonely, winter was dark, and my phone sat silent. I was home with our one baby. It felt like an unbearable struggle with no end in sight and all I could do was cry or pray. I had the choice to live in despair or offer up a sacrifice of praise. I gave into despair and crumbled in defeat many days, but God wasn't done working. My feelings of unbelief dictated my days. I was a woman of faith, but I had not yet grasped true freedom available in Christ for myself. I believed we were just sinners always meant to struggle with sin and live in dreary doom our whole life.

In part, that is true. We will wrestle with the battle of flesh and spirit as long as we have breath, but what we do with the struggle is what matters. We can put our hope in the One who is more than capable of healing us and died to set us free. We can touch the hem of Jesus in faith or stand up when he tells us to stand. We have the choice to utilize the tools in scripture and to pray scripture. Fasting is an example of a powerful tool that often goes unnoticed. We don't have to suffer our whole lives. We can find freedom.

There was a woman who was bleeding for twelve years (Luke 8:43-48 NLT) and a man who was lame for thirty-eight years (John 5:1-15 NLT). Maybe they pushed every door and asked for help from everyone they knew. We don't know what their journey was like, but we can assume both held on to hope all those years, waiting for a Messiah to come heal them and set them free. I'm sure there were days of discouragement and despair. They didn't have modern medicine or know about miracle healings yet.

Jesus wasn't ministering to the towns yet, but when He arrived, their faith was ripe and ready to receive. They were ready to be healed. Their hearts were soft and ready to believe that Jesus would heal them. The woman had been an outcast for several years, considered to be dirty in her culture. She didn't just go away for a few days each month; she was hidden and isolated from people for twelve years. She was desperate and lonely. When she heard Jesus, the Teacher was speaking in her town, she knew she had to go to him. If only she could just touch the hem of his garment, she was certain she would be healed. She believed it in her heart. If only she could get close enough to Him, He would help her. She was overflowing with years of hope and bursting with desperation to be noticed and cared for. Jesus felt the power of healing go out of Him, and He knew there was someone near with the faith to be healed.

There was a man who was lame and could not walk for thirty-eight years.

Was he born with a disability?

Maybe.

Was it self-inflicted pain and he was just being lazy, refusing to walk?

I wouldn't think so.

We don't know the cause of his inability to move, but we do know there was a pool only a few feet away that was thought to have had healing properties, and he kept hoping someone would help him to the pool. If only he could get close enough to be first to the pool, he was certain he would be healed. That is a long time to hope. That's a long time to wait for someone to help. When a man with a kind voice came up to him and asked, "Would you like to be well?" the lame man could have doubted and waved Jesus away as a crazy person or he could have said, "No, thanks I'll wait for someone else to help me up." But he didn't.

He listened and stood up. He was instantly healed. He was desperate, and he was ready to be healed.

We get some insight into the possible cause of his sickness. Later Jesus finds him in the temple and tells him to stop sinning or something worse will happen to him. Maybe he was living in sin thirty-eight years prior and it had caused a sickness that could not be healed. Maybe it was an exceptionally long natural consequence to that sin and stubbornness to repent. We don't know the whole story but Jesus saw him.

We can choose to live in sin our whole lives, just hoping for freedom. We have the choice to drudge our way through the same perpetual struggles just hoping for healing. The truth is that Jesus already came. He already set the captives free. The bleeding woman and the lame man spent years waiting for hope of healing that came in a way that is offered to each of us every day, a gift offered right in front of us. We do not have to suffer for twelve years or sit like a limp noodle for thirty-eight years waiting for healing to come. There is a choice right in front of us. When God said we have every tool we need in His word, it may seem mysterious, but the secret is no secret. We really do have every tool we need offered to us in the Word of God.

The Enemy has strategized in society to twist the purpose of fasting and lead people to believe fasting exists for self-improvement. We can abstain from sugar, screen time, or Sunday football and call it a fast. We can do a smoothie cleanse and give up certain foods to achieve better health and call it a fast, but like any tool God placed in Scripture, fasting has a purpose and it is for our good. Giving up screen time or skipping sports on Sunday afternoon is removing an idol of our heart. God sees the heart. He sees our motive and what may be dictating our day. If we have an unrepentant heart with lurking sins, God can't hear our fasting and prayers. He can see the hidden motives. There are several types of fasts throughout the Bible we can learn from. The Elijah fast (1 Kings 19, NLT) teaches us to break negative mental and emotional habits. The Samuel fast (1 Samuel 7:1-12 NLT) teaches us to pray for revival and winning souls. The Disciples' fast (Matthew 9:1-8 NLT) teaches us to deal with sins and bondages we can't break through with prayer alone. This fast helps us to overcome the struggle, conquer bitterness toward others, and weed out the pride.

Fasting reflects our inner desires by our outward discipline. We can give up shopping for a month, but what is the motive behind it? If it is simply to save money, that is not going to change anything. But if God is convicting your heart of your spending habits and is asking you to obey by giving up shopping for a month, you are taking control over the sin instead of the sin controlling you. By fasting food, we are taking control over our fleshly desires and bringing our sin and pride under the lordship of God. He then can do the spiritual work in our hearts to break those strongholds. We are essentially saying "I choose you God, I choose to deny my desire to eat right now and spend that time with you." He honors our decision to choose Him and our faith is strengthened.

The stronger the sin, the more often we may need to fast. As we commit to the fast, our faith grows stronger as we eagerly anticipate God's answer. We are strengthened and renewed in our fervor to believe God will do what He says He will do. He will show up. He is the Source of revival in our hearts and as we discipline ourselves to prayer and fasting, He is faithful to fulfill His promises. That doesn't mean we will have a problem-free life. The Enemy will still throw rocks on the road and search for cracks to sneak in and steal our joy, but we continue fighting. God is on our side, and He has given us all we need to face any trial that comes.

We face new seasons, new years, and new rhythms all the time. We have the opportunity to learn what God wants to teach us in a season, and then it is time to pack up the decorations and move forward. We also have the choice to sit in the same spot staring at last year's Christmas tree. It will be withered and dead. Like Proverbs 26:11 (NLT) says, we can be fools like a dog who returns to his own vomit. We can move forward to seek out the tools God knew we would need and prepared for us in Scripture to help us live an abundant life. Jesus died so we could have access to those tools, and when we seek scripture, the Holy Spirit helps us find what we need. We were made to glorify God with our lives and to reflect His beauty and character just as the moon reflects the light of the sun. The moon is constant and unchanging, and though we can't be constant, we can be changing.

We can be ever-changing and transforming day by day if we choose to use the tools God has given us. We can feel like we are just plodding along but still be faithfully allowing God to teach us and change us in each season. If we refuse to obey His voice or come under His authority, He will bring that lesson back around in another season because He is long-suffering and perfectly content to keep teaching us. He has all the time in the world, but we don't. We only have one life to live, and His heart is for us to grasp how deep, how wide, how high His love was when He sacrificed His son on the cross so we could live in freedom and embrace the life He has given us today.

I imagine it grieves His heart to see His children squandering away that sacrifice or letting life go by believing there is no freedom from sin. We can repent and come to Him any time. The Bible says, "There is no condemnation for those who belong to Christ" (Romans 8:1 NLT). He is a good God, a loving God who wants to correct those He loves. He allows us to walk through refining fires so we can come out as purified gold. He loves tending to us and making us more beautiful, no matter how long it takes. He is in no hurry for us to learn the hard truth or accept His blessings. He would love for us to receive the freedom and healing instantly like the lame man, but He leaves the choice up to us if we want to yield in the moment or not.

His heart is to transform us into the likeness of Christ, and He gets our attention through trials, seasons of suffering, or refining circumstances. He bubbles up those perpetual sins to the surface so we have the chance to draw closer to Himself and be changed. If we are willing to be moldable in His hands, then He is faithful to heal us and help us to overcome. We have the choice to go to Him for healing so our life doesn't pass by while we sit paralyzed.

He wants us to be healed, focused, and useful so we are enabled to reach more people with the time we are given. God's heart is for all people to come to Him and He uses us, His children, to reach the lost and the lonely.

I can't reach people that you can reach, and you can't reach people that I am in relationships with. We all have different jobs, families, and circles of influence for a reason. We all have different gifts and strengths and ways to bless those who come into our path. If we sit silently and stay home, Satan wins. He keeps us paralyzed from seeking the truth of Jesus and finding the tools that will free us. It is his mission as he prowls around looking for lives to destroy, to keep all God's blessings and treasures hidden.

So often I have come across churchgoers who sit in their seats week after week never seeing the power and presence of God right in front of them. If only they would turn their eyes to Him and open their hearts to see. They sit there missing the very abundant blessings He wants to pour over them. They disregard a season of struggle and push away the hard parts of life instead of pressing in to see the treasure within. I wonder if there were other women with "continual bleeding" who chose to stay hidden in their house and died of loneliness, or other paralyzed men by the pool who did not want to stand up.

Our sins can be conquered, and struggles can be overcome. A different sin may come up and we may struggle again, but every time it comes up, we have a choice. Every moment we recognize our sin, we have the same choice before us to confront it and confess it or let it control us.

We were made to worship God and glorify Him. We were made to be His vessels and witnesses in this world to build His kingdom. He wants us to conquer sin and overcome the struggle so we can be more useful to Him. Instead of sin constantly bubbling up and paralyzing us, we can confront it, and the zeal for the Lord can bubble out of us. He replaces the sin struggle with fresh soil, and He plants new growth if we allow Him. He fills us with the power of the Holy Spirit so we can go out into the world sharing the Good News of what He has done.

If that pot is shattered, He is going to start gluing the pieces back together. If that fruit tree needs pruning, He is going to get out His pruning shears and start cutting. He is a faithful God of constant restoration and repair. When we cry out for help, He will come to the rescue. That is what

He does. If we call on the name of the Lord, He will be there. If we need comfort, He will cover us with His wing. Neglected gardens get weeds, but there is still growth. Broken hearts shed tears, but there is still beauty. Roses have sharp thorns, but there is still a flower. The woman who had perpetual bleeding for twelve years or the lame man who suffered for thirty-eight years both faithfully held onto hope. When the time came for healing, they wanted to be healed. God is asking the question in this new season: "Would you like to get well?" (John 5:1-15 NLT)

We have to be willing to do the hard work and seek scripture to find the tools we need. Are we willing to root out the sin and confess to a sister or brother in Christ? We have to do the faithful, steady work of abiding in Him and obeying His voice when He is leading us out of our comfort. If we can't hear His voice, we need to start eliminating the excess in our lives. If there is a sin or perpetual struggle you can't seem to conquer, you have to be willing to do whatever it takes. So often in scripture, the immediate action step is fasting. It seems to be an automatic response. Over the generations, the tool of fasting has slowly been hidden from God's people as cultural norms have piled up with distractions and noise. The weight can feel unbearable, and we were not meant to carry that pile. It may be time to repent and remove that pile, tuning your heart into God and hearing His voice. There are tools to help and heal us, and God is always leaving the choice up to us to go to His Word and dig for the tool we need for that day.

Are you willing to do whatever it takes to uproot that perpetual struggle?

Will you lay face down fully surrendered to the Lord?

Think of a way to grow that intimacy with the Lord today. Write it down.

### Action step #6:

Go to your local garden center, get a small plant, and take care of it. Water it, give it sunshine, and recognize that this plant signifies your spiritual walk. Your soul needs diligent care too. Read John 5:1-15 and ask yourself the honest question — Do I want to be well? Spend some time journaling an honest answer to that question and what may be hindering that growth. Let your mind wander for a while in your journal and get out gel pens or colored pencils to doodle something lovely. Your Notice Notebook is going to be a treasure to look back on one day. I have a tote of them and it is so refreshing on the occasional days I climb up my attic stairs to be reminded of God's goodness throughout my life.

# DO YOU WANT TO BE WELL?

*beauty among the thorns*

**STAY FAITHFUL TO THE PATH THE LORD HAS SET YOU ON.**

This little scene reminded me of the story of Gideon (Judges 6-7), a small but mighty army of 300 soldiers with humble hearts, bending over water to take their last drink before going into battle. Bees are a small but mighty force in nature, they stick together working as one unified organism to accomplish something extraordinary.

# chapter 7

There were some cold winters in the Midwest, and with a third baby coming, I needed a warm escape. We booked our flights to an island in South Carolina, and while we were packing, my husband announced that he had spontaneously sent out a few resumes to companies at the location we were flying to. I didn't think much of it, and while we were there vacationing, I was in the emergency room getting a piece of dirt removed from behind my eye, when he got a call from an employer to set up an interview. Ironically it worked out to meet with him later that same day and a couple of weeks later, the awaited phone call came and he got the job. Five months later with a newborn baby and two toddlers in tow, we were driving across the country to an unfamiliar island where we didn't know anyone. We kept repeating "Okay, Lord, one more step." Within the first month, a hurricane hit, and we had to evacuate; a week later we came back to a destroyed island, and time was running out on the rental. We needed to find a home. "Okay, Lord, one more step." My mind was swirling, and my heart was a raging hurricane of emotion. I was obeying God's leading—why was every step such a battle?

The Lord opened the right house at the right time, and we moved in fast. We settled into the new neighborhood and started visiting churches. We were quickly recognizing how apparent it was that God seemed to be doing a much bigger work moving us across the country than we could comprehend at the time and was bringing many families to the area, all with similar stories of leaving homes and families behind, but all the pieces felt like a scattered mess. All we could do was trust Him with one more step each day.

I was going to mom groups and Bible studies, but I never seemed to be fitting in anywhere. I was discouraged and barely held it together with three tiny toddlers. One morning, I mustered up my last bit of courage and visited a mom's Bible study group, only to be completely ignored. They had no idea the hurricane of emotions swirling in my heart and the eruption of tears I was holding back. I say all this to show the dark pit of despair I was allowing myself to fall into; I was clambering to stay afloat and catch my breath. I was unsettled and clinging to my faith, but the desperation was intensifying to find the reason why the Lord had brought us all the way across the country only to struggle so much. It didn't make sense. I relented. I resolved to be content in this season of loneliness and venture out to enjoy the beautiful weather with my little ones.

We tried a new playground, and this lovely friend breezed into my life like a breath of fresh air in what seemed to be God's perfect timing. We became sisters overnight, diving deep into the stories of our lives—our families quickly grew close. I latched onto her like I had found water in the desert. She brought me to a prayer group with women who all treated each other like sisters, hugging each other as if a week felt like a year. The love for each other was apparent, and I felt safe enough my first night there to let the floodgates of tears gush out. In the moment, they surrounded me with prayers and hugs, and they offered a hand of support by sending a cleaning crew. They jumped to meet the immediate need, but then I didn't hear from them and they didn't reciprocate my efforts to reach out. The friendships outside the group weren't forming. However, I was determined to give it a real chance and open my heart to this group. I went week after week, getting closer to the friend who brought me, and tried making connections with the other women, but then I started noticing something was not right in the prayer time. I was sensing something was off, discerning whether a message was from the Spirit of God or from another spirit. There were teachings that didn't line up with Scripture, songs being played that were produced out of heretical churches, and I started to see the Spirit of God was being distorted. It was loud and repetitive, a hypnotic worship that was putting the women into a trance-like state. The true God of the Bible is peaceful and gentle. He takes notice of others and cares deeply. We were made to worship Him with our whole heart and then love others. It's His greatest commandment. We should be coming together to worship our heavenly Father and leaving refreshed by His peaceful presence. My convictions were starting to scream over the noise, and I couldn't stay silent. The warning signs were clear and I spoke up about the falsehood when there were opportunities. I would put together more worshipful playlists that pointed to the Lord when it was my week and they would turn up the volume and press into the rhythmic meditations. There are certainly times for dancing and joy in the Lord but this group seemed to be more about emotional stimulation while there was evident prayer needs going unnoticed. I was seeing a picture of what the true gospel was not and I had to walk away from the group. The sisterly friend I grew to care deeply about did not see it the way I was seeing it, and the friendship ended abruptly. She stopped responding and cut off contact. The very thing my heart longed for was taken away when I was following my personal convictions.

It was the most painful ending to any friendship I had ever known, and the loss had a profound effect on me. I was left with a deep crater, and my reaction to the rejection surprised me. I was desperately clinging onto every thread of hope, and my struggle was going unnoticed. She had chosen to cut off the friendship.

I kept coming back to Romans: "Don't just pretend to love others. Really love them. Hate what is wrong. Hold tightly to what is good. Love each other with genuine affection and take delight in honoring each other" (Rom. 12:9-10 NLT). It wasn't the true Spirit of God to abandon a sister in her struggle. That was not the gospel of Jesus. I left the group and there was radio silence from all of my sisters there.

I love when scripture says "but"—it means God is about to speak hope. Here is my "but" in the bottom of that crater, I discovered some deep-rooted sins in my own heart that God wanted to purify and He used that loss to reveal my void. I was more alone than ever before but growing closer to the Lord. I was learning down there in the crater of that season who the true Jesus was. I was learning from Scripture, and He was the One who was gently scooping fresh dirt to fill in that hole.

There was one Saturday morning I got so fed up with the swirling emotions that I got a shovel and started aggressively digging out a stubborn, sawtooth palmetto bush in the front yard of our perfectly pristine neighborhood. I was probably digging for a solid two hours in the southern sun, neighbors walking by glaring at my mental breakdown, but I didn't care. Those roots–physical and sinful–were coming out. I stood there staring over the physical crater, and I came face to face with the truth that God purifies us through fire. Purification is a continual peeling away and pruning process. According to Webster's dictionary, "sanctification is a fancy word for being freed from sin or purified, to set apart to a sacred purpose or to religious use." It is the process of being freed. Facing that crater with myself revealed I was clinging to people and not relying on God.

The Lord, in His mercy, was protecting me from being swept up in false teaching and using those circumstances to uproot sins that might not have been revealed any other way. In Romans 12, Paul describes a kind of love that is tightly knit, a love so deep it is unbreakable, a love that is warm and kind, an intimate spiritual communion or koinonia. God designed us to be in this intimate, loving community as a body of believers all actively using our giftings to help one another. We can't walk in our spiritual giftings and nurture a healthy family of believers if we have rotten roots. We must first be purified in our hearts, strengthened in our faith, and growing in maturity. In His mercy, God brings us on that path of victory and freedom one step at a time, and He seems to use broken people or seasons of suffering to refine us.

Paul teaches us in 1 Corinthians about spiritual gifts. With urgency, he says, "I plead with you." He is pleading with the people of Rome to give their bodies to God for all He has done for them. He says, "Do not copy the behavior and customs of this world, but let God transform you into a new person by changing the way you think. Then you will learn to know God's will for you, which is good and pleasing and perfect" (Rom. 12:1-2 NLT). He speaks with a yearning for the people to be purified and transformed. He is teaching us to be a living sacrifice to God. Our sinful nature entangles us and blinds us from seeing God's pleasing and perfect will. He wants us to step out in obedience and yield to the refining fires. He promises good will come from the fire; like silver is refined through fire, we are refined through suffering.

Paul warns the people to know the true Spirit of God. There will be people with the wrong spirit claiming they know God, but they don't know the true God who is gentle and kind and steadfast in our suffering, the God who genuinely cares for His people and is a true friend in all seasons. We can accept Jesus as Lord of our life and still go through life not knowing the Spirit of God. His heart is to purify us so we can see Him. "Blessed are the pure in heart for they will see God" (Matt. 5:8 NLT). The more we yield to His refining process, the more we will see Him. My heart hungers and thirsts for His righteousness (Matt. 6:33 NLT) and longs to see Him. I allowed Him to painfully dig up those deep rotten roots, and He began to fill that crater back in with healthy, rich soil. My husband sat on the rocking chair watching me struggle and toil, knowing I needed to sweat it out, and in the end, he took me in his arms and just held me. I knew it was all going to be okay and that we were in the palm of God's hand. He was with us, purifying my unclean heart. He has a good plan in our suffering so we will become more useful in His kingdom purposes and our gifting to be more refined.

The Holy Spirit gives us all different gifts to help each other. If one person is given the gift of healing but sits there quietly, there could be a sister among them who never receives the healing prayer she needs. If one person is given the ability to give wise advice but never speaks up, the rest of the body of believers misses the correction and blessing. The gifts of the Holy Spirit are meant to build up the body, encourage and strengthen. Paul teaches that the Holy Spirit gives the ability to discern whether a message is from the Spirit of God or from another spirit. If it's tearing down or confusing, it is not from God. Paul was saying: don't misunderstand this, don't miss this, tune in and listen closely (1 Cor. 12:1 NLT). There has come a day when the true Spirit of God is often confused for other spirits. "You know that when you were still pagans, you were led astray and swept along in worshiping speechless idols" (1 Cor. 12:2 NLT). Many Christians sitting in churches today, going through the rhythm and routine, are completely unaware and do not realize how slow-boiled and deceived they have become. The Spirit of God has faded to the background and many have forgotten their true love of when they first saw the light of Jesus. God's heart is for us to have faith like children and be purified so we can see Him and be one of the many parts making up the whole body of believers.

We are to help each other, love each other, speak out with boldness, pray in faith, prophesy, and be courageous and unashamed in stepping out to obey what the Holy Spirit is leading us to do. If there is a weaker part in the group, we should be strong enough to lift that one up. We ought to be so tightly knit together that we fight to protect each other as we protect ourselves. We are to protect ourselves against deceptions and false teaching sneaking in. When I brought attention to the false teaching, it should have been welcomed with an eagerness to learn more. Paul teaches many groups throughout scripture and gives urgent warnings to protect people from false idol worship. In Galatians, he says, "I am shocked that you are turning away so  soon from God, who called you to himself through the loving mercy of Christ. You are following a different way that pretends to be the Good News but is not the Good News at all. You are being fooled by those who deliberately twist the truth concerning Christ. Let God's curse fall on anyone, including us or even an angel from heaven who preaches a different kind of Good News than the one we preached to you" (Gal. 1:6-8 NLT). And then Paul repeats himself to be sure it was heard. He is warning them like a mama would warn her child—do not touch the stovetop, it will be hot and burn your hand. Why little children look directly at mama and hear her but still have to touch the stove, I don't know, but here we must listen and heed Paul's teaching.

I have no doubt the hearts of those women in my prayer group loved the Lord with all their hearts, but some were aligning themselves with a wrong spirit, false teachers, and the fruit of their actions was showing. If we are to protect ourselves against any other version of the Good News, then we must be careful who we are listening to and what voices we align ourselves with. In our world of social media, books, authors, and conferences galore, there are a lot of voices. Don't follow my voice in these pages. Listen for God's still quiet voice. Open your Bible and learn to hear His voice through Holy scripture. David the Psalmist says, "The words of the Lord are flawless, like silver purified in a crucible, like gold refined seven times" (Ps. 12:6 NLT). How will we know when it is the wrong voice? We have to know the voice of our Shepherd, Jesus, and have an intimate personal relationship with him. We have to spend time in God's Word to get to know Him. Jesus says in John 10:27-28 (NLT), "My sheep listen to my voice; I know them, and they follow me. I give them eternal life, and they will never perish. No one can snatch them away from me." Does he know you as one of his sheep?

The more time we spend in stillness and crave knowledge from the Word of God, the more we can see clearly. If we are applying what Scripture says, even if it is one verse at a time, we will grow so hungry for more and more, and then we find those holes filled in with fresh soil and those areas of brokenness restored. The Holy Spirit breathes new life into us and inspires us with new ideas—art to create and words to share that will bless others. We are to become healed and whole ourselves so we can go out and fully love others; for as long as we have breath, we are to bee a blessing. In the humility of our own brokenness, we can offer that same healing to others that Jesus gave us. Let Him purify your heart.

We will always be imperfect, flawed beings. I am a broken pot with many cracks. I have my struggles and stammers, but my heart cries out with the ardor to know God more fully and to see His face. I'm not willing to live in the puddle of being a hopeless sinner my whole life. David was a sinner; he murdered another man and committed adultery with Bathsheba, yet when he came face to face with his sin, he chose humility and repentance. "Have mercy on me, O God, because of your unfailing love. Because of your great compassion, blot out the stain of my sins. Wash me clean from my guilt. Purify me from my sin. I recognize my rebellion; it haunts me day and night" (Ps. 51:1-3 NLT).

My heart longs to see His mighty mercies poured out, and it's in that heart cry where my heart will be purified. I love reading David's words. He didn't hold back his heart cry. He wasn't ashamed of anyone hearing the longing of his heart. He was so poetic and vulnerable, letting the words tumble out of his soul like a free-flowing river, crying out to be washed whiter than snow and to be given back his joy again. He was broken and crying out to rejoice again, desperate for a clean heart and renew a loyal spirit (Ps. 51:10 NLT). I can almost hear his weeping through the pages of Scripture, begging God not to banish him from His presence and take away the Holy Spirit from him. He longed to be restored and willing to obey. "The sacrifice God desires is a broken spirit. You will not reject a broken and repentant heart, O God" (Ps. 51:17 NLT).

Our brokenness should move us to His mercy where He forgives and our joy is restored. Then David went out to teach God's mercy and ways to rebels so they would return to God (Ps. 51:13 NLT). Weeds pop up in the garden of our hearts, and we can let those weeds take over, lock the gate, and throw away the key, never to delight in the garden again. Weeds of bitterness, pride, and addiction need to be uprooted, or they can all take over and tie us down. Weeds can be seeing a certain name calling on your phone and your response is to push end or let time pass by, holding onto the same hurt feeling. Our pride can prevent us from picking up the phone and time can pass by. We can be willing, though, to fight our way out and follow the path to the root cause of our bitter response or angry outburst.

Our reaction and what comes out of our mouth reveals what is in our heart (Matthew 12:34b NLT). There is always a cause at the root of the reaction, and there is always a way out toward healing. Always. It should compel us to go to God and cry out for His mercy to show us our sin so we can be freed from it. We were already freed from it when Jesus hung on the cross, so why should we waste our day dwelling on it? When we can't find the words to pray or the poetic words to pour out feelings, we have 150 Psalms to turn to and let the cleansing tears flow. Praise the Lord!

"May the words of my mouth, and the meditations of my heart be pleasing to you, O Lord, my rock and my redeemer" (Psalm 19:14 NLT). We were made to praise the Lord. Praise flows from our grateful hearts. If praise is being blocked or neglected, there is a reason and a root. God knows the power of praise is not to just give Him glory but to also break the blockage in our hearts. Praise creates in us the bubbling up of joy and the wellspring of life. Even if you don't feel like praising, you can still choose to say, "Praise the Lord!" Say it over and over if you need to until the heaviness weighing on your heart lifts. Jesus gave us the gift of praise, and as we spend time in God's word and praising Him, our hearts are purified.

Say the words right now, "Praise the Lord!"

Is there something holding you back from speaking it out loud?

Are you willing to be purified?

**Action step #7.**

Run until you break a sweat, take a polar plunge, or smash a pot. Let God stretch you to your limits. His mercy breaks us down so we can be built back up stronger. Sometimes we need a physical "digging up palm roots" action step to jolt our senses before God finally has our attention. It might be helpful to glue the pieces of the pot you just broke back together. Plant your favorite flower and let it be a reminder of how you serve the God who restores our brokenness and fills our cracks. Your beauty is blooming more each day, my friend. Stay faithful to the course as He refines and purifies you. It may be painful at the moment but it leads to the best gift, I promise.

# Purify my heart

"SEARCH ME, GOD, AND KNOW MY HEART; TEST ME AND KNOW MY ANXIOUS THOUGHTS. POINT OUT ANYTHING IN ME THAT OFFENDS YOU, AND LEAD ME ALONG THE PATH OF EVERLASTING."
PSALM 139:23-24 NLT

WHAT IS HOLDING YOU BACK? ASK THE LORD TO REFINE YOUR HEART.

# chapter 8

A woman's heart is an intricately designed thousand-piece puzzle. It takes time to create a masterpiece, and God takes great care piecing together each life. He is not in a hurry. He wants our heart and to bring us back to wholeness. We can genuinely strive to follow Jesus while we walk wounded. The human heart is the most deceitful of all things, and desperately wicked (Jeremiah 17:9 NLT) and the distractions of our day can lead us astray, but the goodness of God continues to draw us back to Himself, always back to the vine (John 15 NLT). When we remain in Him, our lives will produce lasting fruit. We still wrestle with the temptation of comparison that imprisons us and we can be held captive in the wilderness of our wandering heart, but God is steadfast and patient with His people. David cries out in the Psalms with a sad heart, discouraged and broken, wandering in grief and loneliness (Psalm 43-44). He yearns for the days of joy when the people were worshiping, but he knows God sees the secrets of every heart and when we get distracted or spread our hands in prayer to foreign gods (Psalm 44:20-21 NLT). God never leaves us. He is so good to continue relentlessly pursuing us. We can settle for a life of despair, but God desires freedom.

The battle for our heart and our soul is very real. Some seasons can be a full-on war. When we surrender our life to Christ, He never said we were setting up a comfortable camp. He said there will be troubles and trials. God doesn't give up or quit working on us. He cares about every life. I have spent much of my life talking about the longing for freedom, to fly free like the birds. I knew what the Bible taught about the freedom we can have in Christ but didn't fully realize the true picture of the gospel. Our enemy loves nothing more than to keep a tight grip on our hearts, using the wounds and rejection of our pasts to keep us caged in. We can be tempted to turn inward and hide in the deep caverns of our heart, but Jesus is there knocking at the door, offering to unlatch the lock and lead us into the beauty outside. We can be gripped with the fear of taking His hand and letting Him lead us into the thorny world where all the pain was inflicted on us. The darkness of loneliness can seem the safer choice; Satan knows our weakness and even if we can muster up enough courage within ourselves to step out into the light, the tiniest bit of rejection can send us scurrying back into our cage where it seems safe. Jesus came to show us another way. He came to take our place on the cross so we could be free and live a wildly abundant life. At some point we must choose to simply obey and let Him lead us in the way of freedom.

As we seek Him with all our heart, He leads the way. On our wedding day, my father's speech was about our last name meaning "outside the camp." We had no idea that phrase was going to be a literal lesson in the years to come. We were set on a winding path through closed doors, walls, and church rejections, but God was leading us one step further outside the camp in every season with a purpose in the suffering. "We glory in our sufferings, because we know that suffering produces perseverance; perseverance, character; and character, hope" (Romans 5:3-4 NIV).

God was about to take us out a step even further, out of our comfortable box. We were finally feeling more settled in our suburban home, or at least learning to be content where the Lord had us. We still had unanswered prayers and longings in our heart for more but we were enjoying where we lived. We could drive our golf cart around town, walk to local festivals, spend our weekends at the pool or beaches. We had several playgrounds within stroller distance, and the Lord added two more babies to our family so we needed those playgrounds. Life was beautiful, what more could we ask for? So here we were, now with five little ones, when Sam came home from work one ordinary day at his usual time and started taking pictures off the walls. The wilderness can feel endless, he had his days of frustration, but he was steady and certain. He said it was time to take a step of faith in obedience and get the house ready to sell. I asked him where we were moving to, and he didn't know. I simply trusted him and got a tote. We were being led further outside our safe box of familiarity. I was holding onto our beautiful home with a white-knuckle grip, it felt secure there and I didn't want to let go of our life of comforts. Three days later, I relented and a mini farm came on the market. Doesn't it seem like God sheds light on the next step the moment we loosen our grip? When God asks, "who will go?" are we ready to say "here I am Lord"? We jumped into the car on a dreary, cold Sunday evening hoping to see the property before it was too dark. It was only an hour away, but it felt like a foreign land. We pulled up to a winding driveway, and around the dark curve was a house tucked back by the creek. It was a muddy puddle mess. We walked into an outdated kitchen; the house was drab with cramped rooms, walls that were never painted after the first coat of dull white primer, stained smelly carpet, and foggy windows; I felt confined and wanted to run far away from that colorless property the instant I walked in. On the way home, Sam could see the bigger picture of vibrant potential and asked me to trust him and make an offer. I had a split moment of decision—was I going to follow my stubborn heart and run far away or was I going to obey that quiet voice nudging me to trust my husband?

We put in an offer and the very next day, it was accepted. This mama of five was in shock–what was happening? How was this happening so fast? Sometimes when it is God's perfect timing, He moves fast and we need to be ready to go. We now had a month to get our house ready to sell, list it, sell it, pack it up and move out. We didn't have the support of a church family, but it felt like God was asking us to step out of the boat and leading us further beyond the comfortable walls to a foreign land. Somewhere deep in my terrified heart, I knew God was working and He was with us in this move, even if it wasn't clear yet.

It was daunting to step out into these unknown waters and leave our familiar behind, but the unknown was becoming more familiar with every step of obedience. Our God is a personal God, and He knows how to lead us in the way He wants us to go. He is going to lead each of us on a unique path toward fulfilling the Great Commission. Jesus said, "Therefore, Go make disciples of all nations" (Matt. 28:16-20 NLT). It is going to look different for each of us if we are living surrendered to following Jesus, and it won't always mean settling into membership at a church or following the direction of that specific church family. It may be a direction you can't imagine. You may already feel a stirring you can't logically describe. God will take great care in showing each of us the way to go. There are times He asks us to say "no" to one thing so we can say "yes" to where He is leading.

When we give our heart fully to Jesus and we are set free from our cage of entrapment, God sets our feet on a new path following Him and His vision of the Bible to reach all people of all nations. We are to learn from Jesus and follow the leading of the Holy Spirit in our lives. God needs Christ followers sent across America and around the world who are willing to sacrificially obey and go where He leads. God alone knows our hearts; He searches our hearts and knows how to direct and lead our path. He doesn't lead us into the wilderness to abandon us. He is not silent in seasons to torment us. He wants our undivided attention. He is a jealous God and wants our whole heart.

When we put our hope in mere humans or rely on human strength, Jeremiah says we are cursed like stunted shrubs in the desert with no hope for the future and living in the barren wilderness in an uninhabited salty land (Jeremiah 17:5-6 NLT). The way of this world can be appealing, and we can be enticed to follow what seems good or even what seems like the logical way to go. Our pride wants to pursue the validation of mere humans, but our roots will continue to grow shallow. Roots that grow wide will flow with the tide but if we put our hope in the Lord, our roots are going to grow deep down in the humble ways of the Lord and the tides won't move us. Jeremiah goes on to say, "But blessed are those who trust in the Lord and have made the Lord their hope and confidence. They are like trees planted along a riverbank, with roots that reach deep into the water. Such trees are not bothered by the heat or worried by long months of drought. Their leaves stay green, and they never stop producing fruit" (Jeremiah 17:7-8 NLT). If our roots are growing deep, we will know we are right where He wants us to be, and we won't be moved when trials come.

Do you want to be a fruitful tree not bothered by heat or worried by drought? My husband moved us far outside our walls of comfort to a dreary property, and then he asked me to trust him with a step even further. He was going to quit his job for six months to remodel the house and upgrade the property full-time. Moving out of our safe neighborhood was a big step, but now he was completely taking away security that comes with income. Did he lose his mind or was he being led by faith? Those six months turned into more than a year of sawdust and chaos, quiet days, and loneliness, but instead of the familiar pain of isolation, Jesus was becoming my close-knit companion. It was stretching into two years before Sam had his own company up and running full-time. I had unsettling days of insecurity homeschooling little ones, and our faith was being stretched to what felt like maximum capacity. But the roots of our tree were growing deeper, and we were discovering an unexpected intimacy with the Lord that was beyond anything we could fathom. He was slowly bringing us out of the stream of worldly ways and teaching us to walk more in the way of faith. He brought us back to the old hymn "At the Cross"—it was there by faith I received my sight. When we walk through valleys, He reminds us we walk by faith, not by sight, and it doesn't always make logical sense at the time.

Obedience can be a sacrifice and it was starting to become a true sacrifice for us, but it was also getting exciting. We were led outside the walls of the institutional Church, outside the walls of our charming southern-style home, outside the walls of a comfortable suburban life to an unfamiliar way of living. It did not make any logical sense on paper, but we were on a journey of learning what it means to live like Jesus outside the camp. Hebrews 13:13 (NLT) says, "Let us, then, go to Jesus outside the camp, bearing the disgrace he bore." Jesus suffered outside the city gate to make the people holy through his own blood. He was outside the camp to love the people who would never be found within city limits. When we start to see the character of who Jesus is, we are set free. "So Jesus said to the Jews who had believed him, 'You are truly my disciples if you remain faithful to my teachings, and you will know the truth, and the truth will set you free'" (John 8:31-32 NLT). Abiding in him and putting our hope in following his ways sets us free. We don't have to live confined within the walls or rules of religion. Jesus came to show us another way.

Jesus was outside the walls when he met the woman at the well (John 4:1-26 NLT). No one else was there, just Him, and soon she walked up. We often find Jesus going away from the crowd, away from the city, even away from his disciples to be still and listen to the Father. They saw him talking to the quiet ones in the crowds. They watched him take notice of those who were rejected by society. Jesus spoke to the Samaritan woman on the outskirts of town. As a Jew, He was breaking the cultural barriers and the unspoken rules to talk to a woman who was an outcast. We can assume her loneliness and rejection by her life choices with men and marriage, but Jesus could see straight to her heart. He knew what she needed. He knew she was struggling and desperate for someone to notice her. He saw she was thirsty and hungry for more than the life she had. She was not satisfied with her life choices and desperately filled the caverns of her heart with the wrong nourishment. Man after man was not satisfying, and her heart longed for more. She wanted a way out but couldn't see a way.

Jesus could see a way. He is the way, and He stepped in as a friend. He cut straight through to her heart and met her deepest need. He cared for her.

Jesus offered her living water so she would never become thirsty again. It says in the gospel of John 4:14 (NLT), "it becomes a fresh, bubbling spring within them, giving them eternal life." Jesus was expressing to the woman the hope of a time coming and that a time would come when true worshipers will worship the Father in Spirit and in truth. The Father is looking for true worshipers who will worship him that way. "For God is Spirit, so those who worship him must worship in Spirit and in truth" (John 4:24 NLT). The woman believed in faith and at once went to share the news with her friends. She was bubbling with the truth and knowledge that the Messiah had come.

Jesus, in his eternal compassion, goes on to paint a picture for his disciples of true nourishment. He says, "My nourishment comes from doing the will of God who sent me, and from finishing his work" (John 4:34 NLT). Our true freedom is found in doing the will of God and following the ways of Jesus. He noticed the needs of others and selflessly stepped in to meet their needs. There was no selfish gain for Him; He was simply caring about others above himself. Then Jesus told the disciples to look around and see that the fields were ripe for harvest. He opened their eyes to all the people around who were suffering and in need of healing, teaching them to notice people looking for hope. The Samaritan woman was struggling, and He brought light into her darkness. She was bubbling up with living water and her soul was fed. Jesus had come. He had noticed her need and offered her hope. He was asking his disciples to wake up and rise to a higher way of living and bring the light of Jesus into dark places.

Our life is valuable to God. The truth is that our lives are valuable for only a brief time. James says, "Your life is like the morning fog—here for a little while—then it's gone" (James 4:14 NLT).

It can bloom into something utterly glorious if we let the Words of the Lord penetrate deep into our hearts and allow the Holy Spirit to work His mysterious, wild, and wonderful plan for our lives. But we have to fight for truth and embrace the struggle to discover the treasure. The treasure I found in the struggle was spiritual freedom in Christ Jesus. It was in those seasons of loneliness that drew me close to Him. He was all I had most days. With little ones at home and my husband away at work, it was on the quiet days where I realized Jesus was all I needed. He was bringing me to a place where I enjoyed the simple things and the simplicity of having just Jesus, just like my early years when I first saw the Light and the burden of my heart rolled away ("At the Cross"). I had a willingness to do challenging heart work and let Him lead. The ways of this world lost its appeal, and I was hungry for more of God. I found true freedom in breaking out of the boxes of familiarity. I was seeing that the true gospel of Jesus was outside the walls of the building and was in us, His people. We are His temple. He dwells within us, and when we begin to grasp that, our eyes are opened to the glorious truth of the gospel. If we are filled with the Holy Spirit within us, it doesn't matter if we are worshiping God in a building or in the backyard.

Jesus is the Cornerstone, and the people are His Church. People who are born again with the Holy Spirit within them are what breathes life into the church. If the people come to church in despair and show up every Sunday with an emptiness behind their eyes without the Spirit breathing new life, the light will go out, life will leave the building and the church will crumble away. These dying churches are fading away without the Holy Spirit breathing new life. Pastors can preach their best motivational sermons and worship bands can shine their best talents leading people to new heights of emotion, but no amount of perfectly planned services can fabricate the true power and compelling of the Holy Spirit. He breathes new life into the people who will naturally go out to build the kingdom by the compelling of the Spirit within them. If we want to reach people with the love of Jesus, we can't radiate the fruits of the Spirit without first being filled with the Holy Spirit, otherwise it becomes an effort in our own strength. Only the Holy Spirit can breathe life, only He can pour out love, joy, peace, patience, kindness, goodness, faithfulness, gentleness, and self-control, and without His power within us we are weak and have nothing to offer.

Women possess the incredible beauty of God, and we are to reflect Him in our own unique ways. But so often women are hidden behind the sadness in their soul or the shame they carry, and that beauty can't shine out. It is disheartening to see Christ-followers walk into church weary and living without the joy of the Lord or the powerful presence of the Holy Spirit exuding from within them. We possess the hope for a dying world. We are the torchbearers bringing light to a dark and hopeless soul. We are the ones to carry that light. There is no one else. That was God's plan to use us, His daughters reflecting His glory. If we are too paralyzed in despair, He can't use us. If Satan has his grip on us, then we stay tied to strongholds. But God isn't done with you. He is pursuing you relentlessly to lead you to uproot lies and break those strongholds.

God used the quiet of our lonely seasons to gently speak to our hearts and breathe life into our lungs. He was continually showing us freedom is found outside the walls and away from distractions. He was telling us to stop beating our heads against the walls and to break out. All throughout history, man has wanted to build fortresses and camps. But God wants us to cross into the land flowing with milk and honey. We need Jesus, and we need the Holy Spirit breathing life into us, or we will deteriorate into an empty shell of a person. When we realize the truth, the truth will set us free.

When we realize the truth that Jesus has already come and that He died on the cross for us, the truth opens the cage to let us out to fly free like a bird. We don't have to stay trapped our whole lives. We can choose to go out. Jesus says it is not only safe to come out, but He is calling us out. He is calling us out of the darkness into marvelous light. If we are afraid to step out, His hand is waiting there for us to grab. If we are afraid to fly, He will teach us. If we are afraid to show Him our broken wing, He can already see it. He will hide us under His wing until we are healed and ready to fly. He heals us as we spend time with Him, sitting in the stillness of His presence and reading His word. We have to be willing to do the hard work of acknowledging our broken wing and letting Him heal it. If we want to be healed, it requires communication.

It is uncomfortable to communicate. It is much easier to recluse into the shell of ourselves and stay in our despair. In our world of self-help and self-actualization, Satan can deceive us to believe we can find the strength within ourselves to be better. We may feel depressed and experience anxiety, panic attacks, or loneliness, and society says it is only normal. Just because the loudest voices say the same thing does not mean it is true. There are churches that have fallen prey to the lie of false doctrines and have led their sheep astray. The stream of society might be preaching truth that sounds good but isn't true at all. We must turn to God's word to see what is actually true. If you're not baptized in the Holy Spirit, ask God to fill you with His Spirit, then you will be given the gift of worshiping Him in Spirit and truth. When you read scripture, you will find the words jumping off the page and see the Word of God is living and breathing, as Paul says in Hebrews 4:12 (NLT), "it is alive and powerful. It is sharper than the sharpest two-edged sword, cutting between soul and spirit, joints from marrow; it exposes our innermost thoughts and desires."

That is when the work becomes uncomfortable, but so much fruit comes from it. It is our human nature to coil away from confronting heart matters. We don't want to be exposed and naked. It is the natural tendency in our sin nature to cover up the shame and hide away. I can open the pages of my life and share these parts of myself with you because I felt exposed and experienced rejection enough times to see the truth behind the curtain. We were made for so much more. We were made to worship God and whatever hinders us from worshiping Him needs to be brought into the light. It might feel like there is no other option or that going to a church building is what we are told to do, but you don't have to show up week after week with the same emptiness behind your eyes. There is a way to satisfy your soul and bring light to your eyes, and it is found in the presence of the Lord. We were made to bring glory to Him with our lives. We are called to look around us to see the ripe fields ready for harvest and to notice the lost and lonely souls longing to be cared for. I learned the true gospel when I started recognizing the same empty eyes in others that I felt in myself for so many years. I was going through all the right motions and faithfully going to a local church every week, but something was missing. I had a deep well that felt completely empty and dry, and the routine of going to a church every Sunday wasn't filling it.

Church after church, we were like the Samaritan woman searching for more. We were searching for Christ-followers who were coming to the cross and walking away in freedom with faith that was alive. We were looking for prayer meetings and teachings on the tools of warfare. We kept praying and asking the Lord to bring other Christ-followers who were not only hearing the good sermon on Sunday and filling their heads with more knowledge but also living out their faith with passion and conviction. All the churches we visited were shallow or dull, and we would go back home discouraged. Where was the sweet presence of the Lord? Where was the Holy Spirit breathing life and joy? We believed we had to be part of the institutional Church to be part of God's Church, but they seemed to be following the latest trends and models that emotionally charged confer-ences were putting out and we were forcing ourselves to fit into the box. I couldn't sit still in the comfortable routine of attending a regimented church knowing God had so much more for His people. It wasn't until I started pursuing God again in my own personal walk with Him and fol-lowed His leading outside the city walls that I found what I was missing. I found that "bubbling joy" again.

The truth we find in Scripture doesn't define where we worship the Father. It can be right at home in your prayer closet or standing over the kitchen sink washing dishes. Jesus spoke to the woman at the well outside the walls, and she found freedom to worship the Messiah who had come. This speaks of a bright hope for us today that we are given the same free-dom to worship outside the walls because of Jesus. It can be leading a Bible study with a small group of people who are hungry to learn His word or planting a home church in your backyard with a few families eager to live as a church family. He is looking for worshipers who will worship the

Father in Spirit and in truth (John 4:24 NLT). We can't miss this point. He is searching for the pure of heart who want to see Him, know Him, and worship Him with all their heart. That means allowing Him to search our heart (Psalm 139:23-24 NLT) and giving Him access to every hidden part. The woman at the well had secrets hidden deep in the innermost parts of her heart, but Jesus exposed those dark secrets and brought them into the light. She left rejoicing. In the same way, He invites us to let him into every part of our heart so those secrets and sorrows that weigh us down can be exposed to the light and we can leave rejoicing. I read the story of the woman at the well, and her bubbling joy gives me a glimpse of the life to come, the Garden of Eden where we will run and not grow weary, Scripture says.

If you are one of those Christ-followers who feels the emptiness inside and knows something is missing, I understand where you are. It doesn't have to stay the same. We were never made to stay the same and live in safety and comfort. The Lord longs for us to bubble up with the joy of who He is. My days are not all sweet honey and bees just because I share this story, but even on the dreariest of days, there is still so much beauty to see in the honey if we slow down and notice. I am simply a woman with a heart cry to see more of God and obey His voice each day. If you find yourself swimming against the stream of culture and sifting through the noise, then you're hearing the voice of God correctly. He doesn't want us to live with our head in the sand and sit in safety waiting for Jesus' return. Draw near to God, keep seeking Him, keep asking, do the next step and stay faithful to the path He is leading you on. I promise you will find the treasure your heart longs for. And God will be faithful to draw near to you. But don't look for a box with a bow. It will just be empty.

Have you given your whole heart to the Lord?

Have you been truly honest with yourself and allowed Him to search your heart?

Do you want to see what the Lord can do with your willing and humble heart?

Are you ready to take the next step of faith?

**Action Step #8**

Fall on your knees before Jesus and let the tears flow. Cry out to God and tell Him you want to be the kind of tree that grows roots deep in the water (Jer. 17:8 NLT). Seek Him with your whole heart. You don't need a person telling you what to do. God is what your heart longs for. He will overcome you with His presence. Sit in holy reverence of His presence and let Him fill you. If you hunger and thirst for His righteousness, He will fill you (Matt. 5:6 NLT). Draw a picture of a tree with an abundance of fruit in your notebook or take a picture of a tree and let your requests be known to Him. There are some incredible trees around if we take the time to notice.

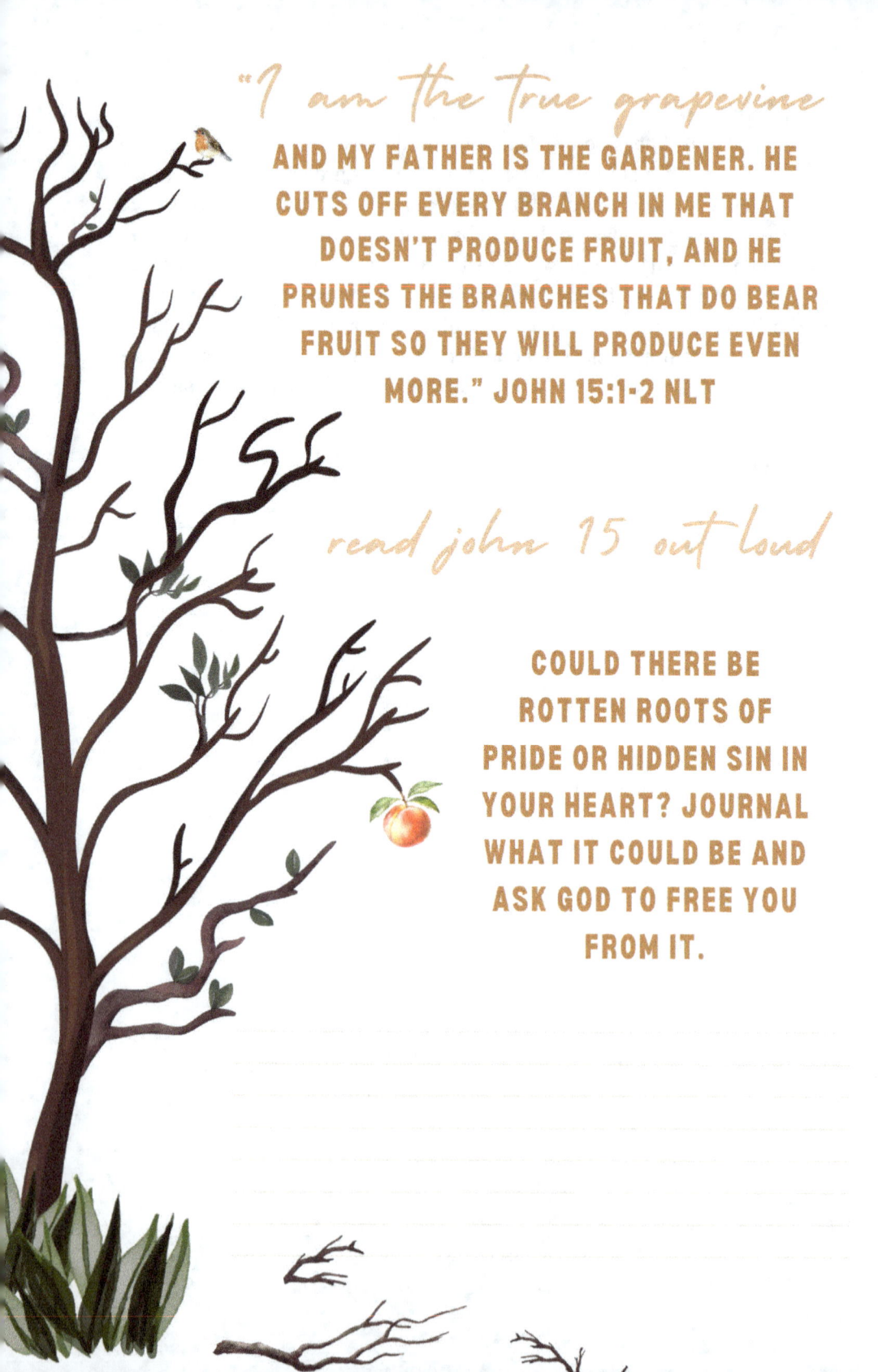

"I am the true grapevine AND MY FATHER IS THE GARDENER. HE CUTS OFF EVERY BRANCH IN ME THAT DOESN'T PRODUCE FRUIT, AND HE PRUNES THE BRANCHES THAT DO BEAR FRUIT SO THEY WILL PRODUCE EVEN MORE." JOHN 15:1-2 NLT

read john 15 out loud

COULD THERE BE ROTTEN ROOTS OF PRIDE OR HIDDEN SIN IN YOUR HEART? JOURNAL WHAT IT COULD BE AND ASK GOD TO FREE YOU FROM IT.

Building my confidence as a new beekeeper working inside the hives.

# chapter 9

I am not naive to the infinite number of different personalities and the millions of pieces that form a life puzzle. I am fully aware my tiny puzzle piece is not the only answer to all people everywhere for all time. But one thing I do know is that you won't find God in a boring brown box. We serve a creative God, and at times, He is wild and mysterious. He is always on the move.

It was Easter Sunday of 2021, and our baby chicks had just hatched a few days before. Our family was in town, and we were gathering for church in our backyard with fourteen family members. Everyone played a part. The older kids read Scripture, the younger kids sang a song, grandparents shared a word of wisdom or knowledge, there was teaching, and we all prayed for each other. There was no band or fanfare, but it was a beautiful picture of the family of believers worshiping together. Grandma came up to me afterwards with a prophetic word the Holy Spirit was prompting her to share—that God wanted to plant a home church on this property one day. I laughed as God is continually working on my unbelief and growing my faith. We were still new to the farm, charging through the mayhem of remodeling and toiling through the isolation. We tried visiting several churches in the area, but every week, it felt like the same scripted order of service. What was the Lord trying to tell us? What were we desperately searching for? Were we selfishly searching for a church to fit our needs? We were being told to find a nice church to plug into but none felt like the right fit.

It turned into a year of quietly walking with the Lord—our little family having church at home together every Sunday with our Bible and a guitar while attempting to teach five small children to sit still for a lesson. Some Sundays were chaotic and filled with tears, and I questioned God in between Sundays–would we be by ourselves another week? It was a lonely season wandering in the wilderness and we were getting to the end of ourselves, but God was faithful to light our path each step of the way. My heart needed that time of stillness to be pruned and prepared. The following Easter, two families asked us on two separate days of the same week if we wanted to meet for a simple service. We looked at each other and just laughed. God's ways are wild and He was working that whole time, we just had to wait on Him. Our three families gathered on our property for a time of worship and prayer. We opened God's word, shared our hearts, and prayed for each other. We grafted two apple tree branches in our front yard as a symbolic lesson that God has grafted us into His family and we are one, unified in the Spirit of the Lord. The church family slowly grew, adding a few more families, but more importantly, God was pruning away dead branches in those with willing hearts, and roots were growing deeper. What God intended to be a fruitful picture of the family of believers, working together for His kingdom purpose, Satan set out from the beginning to destroy.

There is nothing Satan hates more than family. When God's people start to walk in freedom, he tries to tighten the chains and steal our joy. We all came together trying to build a family with our own perspectives, ideas, doctrines, and ways we think church should be and how it should be led. We were questioning our personal ideologies of the Church and what the Bible says church should be, but it always came back to the foundation of what the Bible says. What does the Bible say is the role of the Holy Spirit? What does the Bible say about how the church should function? It was an uncommon way of gathering for church and blazing a new path will zap the strength of even the most secure believer. Every week our faith was being refined and our core values were being sifted. We could no longer be an anonymous face in the crowd or hide behind a mask. We were peeling back the layers, confronting the baggage, and it was uncomfortable. We can have the best intentions to be a unified family by being a willing vessel for God's kingdom purposes, but His ways are far beyond anything we can imagine (Isaiah 55:8-9 NLT) and it doesn't always work the way we think it will.

The unity of the family was growing weak and dividing, and I was helpless to stop it from unraveling, but God was not done working with His people. He cares about every life, and He relentlessly pursues the hearts of His children, even the most stubborn parts. "I am certain that God, who began the good work within you, will continue his work until it is finally finished on the day when Christ Jesus returns" (Philippians 1:6 NLT). Satan will not hesitate to attack the very thing God wants to restore. We must be deeply rooted in the truth of His wild and mysterious ways, or the unity of the family will fray. The Lord led us outside the familiar walls of the organization and He set before us the task of forming a family. There were still people on the island being held captive in the darkness and we serve a God who is in the business of breaking chains and setting the captives free. He was telling us to stay the course no matter how unsteady it seemed.

We all hear from God in different forms, and we all have a unique purpose with different jobs to do and people to love. Jesus spent time with the Father each morning to talk with Him and go where He led. When we get to the end of ourselves and fall on our face in surrender, God meets us there. He begins to show us the unique ways we are to serve in His kingdom purpose if we are willing to be humbled and follow the ways of Jesus. We are all faced with the same daily choice to stay where it is familiar or follow God's voice. Jesus lived in a way that defied logic and modeled a wild way of loving. He called the disciples to follow by faith and blazed a new way of living that was different to the way they had known. He was breaking the yoke of religion with the Pharisees and shattering their ways of thinking.

Jesus told the people, specifically the Samaritan woman here, there was a time coming when it would no longer matter whether you worship the Father on this mountain or in Jerusalem (John 4:21 NLT). He was talking to people familiar with living by the law and being stuck to the routine of sacrifice. But Jesus was describing a way of life that defied all they knew and practiced. He hadn't left us with our Helper, the Holy Spirit, yet and the people didn't yet understand the freedom Jesus would give us through his sacrifice at the cross. We have the power of the Holy Spirit today, yet many churches have become stale and stuck on routine, elevating doctrine without acknowledging the Holy Spirit. It is crucial to evaluate the fruit of the leaders. They are not always aligned with God's word and led by the Spirit. Ministry degrees and pastoral titles don't always qualify a person to lead a flock in Godly ways. I spent six years in ministry school and know the temptation of merely regurgitating head knowledge for the test. We must be discerning whose voice we are listening to. It may be time to break those boxes of doctrine, set aside those theology books, and let God lead you on a new path, the path He has specifically for your life. You don't have to live under that yoke of religion anymore. Be warned, though! It is uncomfortable to break out of the box you have grown accus-tomed to living within, and you might look weird and wild. God's ways are wild and great faith asks you to be wild sometimes. Peter walked on water. That is pretty wild. I realize breaking away from the familiar will make some of you feel uneasy, and I'm saying this more in a metaphorical way. I understand some find great depths of God in theology books and some genuinely love their church family. That is a wonderful thing. They are not evil or wrong in themselves if that is where God has planted you. There are some wonderful churches doing exactly what God wills them to do and people obeying what they are called to do. But if He is leading you outside the walls to plant a church or fly across the globe to reach a group of unreached people, a wild woman with great faith will obey and let Him lead the way. A wild horse running free is one of the most beautiful animals to watch when they are truly free, but once they are tamed and bridled, their spirits break. We can become like a bridled horse with a broken spirit if we're deceived by the wrong voices and fall into the routine of religion. That isn't God's desire for us.

He longs for us to be right with Him and the first step could be a simple act of obedience in forgiving someone. It is simple but it's not easy. The Lord can't speak to you until your heart is right with Him, and maybe He wants you to stay right where you are but you can't move forward until you're at peace with others. He wants your wild heart, your great faith, your radical obedience, and your willingness to serve Him. If you believe what Jesus has done for you on the cross, then it is no longer about the law or the religion, it is about the personal relationship we can have with God the Father. He gives us a new heart; He makes us a new creation. The old life is gone, a new life has begun! (2 Cor. 5:16-17 NLT) It won't be a chore to follow Him. The disciples didn't push Peter out of the boat, his faith moved him over the side of the boat to walk toward Jesus (Matt. 14:29). We will want to honor His commands and joyfully follow the path He lays out.

The warmth and tenderness of God can melt the hardest of hearts and breathe life into the shadows of your soul. Grab hold of His hand and let Him pull you out. If you are still too weak for that, reach out and touch the hem of His garment and He will know you are there (Mark 5:21-34 NLT). He knows everything. He sees every part of you, and the beautiful part of that is He still loves you. He is not like the humans you may have known who have rejected you or didn't notice when you were all alone in your suffering. He is with you in suffering. He isn't like anyone you have ever known. He has a wild way of loving, and His mercy is never-ending.

You cannot define Him or put Him in a box. You can't fully know Him. Paul teaches us in 1 Corinthians 13 that our knowledge is partial and incomplete, and even the gift of prophecy reveals only part of the whole picture. God knows us fully and completely, and one day we will see with perfect clarity. He tells us we used to be children and thought like children (1 Cor. 13:11-12 NLT), but then we grew up and can only see imperfectly as in a cloudy mirror. That is why, I believe, Paul is teaching us with such a deep sense of urgency to get our lives right with Christ and let the Holy Spirit lead us so we can live fully in the ways our Father longs for us to live. Paul didn't care if he was on the road or in prison; he was following where the Father led him to go preach and reach the lost souls he was meant to reach. He is urging us to live with eternal purpose in mind and showing us the only things that last forever are faith, hope, and love, and the greatest of these is love (1 Cor. 13:13 NLT). Are we loving our spouse well? Are we modeling a loving, warm heart for our children? Is God's love bubbling out for the lost to see? Do we notice when our own brothers or sisters in Christ are struggling and love them? Nothing will meet the needs of people more profoundly than the wild love of Christ and we are to be His hands and feet. What is hindering us if we're not loving in that way?

If we are overflowing with love the Holy Spirit gives, then it will bubble out of us and pour out onto those around us. It is a wild way of living that goes against the stream of society, and that current is only going to get stronger to swim against as time goes on. Nowhere in the Bible does it say this life will get easier—quite the contrary—and we need to be the kind of woman who laughs without fear of the future (Proverbs 31:25 NLT), who is right with the Lord and ready to stand firm.

When the market crashes or schemes of man unleash pandemics or the storms of life hit, the people flowing in the stream of society will be surprised at what is happening, and they will feel hoodwinked at the news. But those who are following the Spirit of the Lord won't be shaken nor will they be afraid. They will have seen it coming, and they won't be wavered by the shifting winds. The word of the Lord is our firm foundation, He is our hope and confidence. Remember Jeremiah tells us our roots are deeply planted like a righteous oak, and we will be ready and prepared when the storms hit. God is with us through every storm, every strategy of evil man, and every scheme of Satan. The Enemy has no power over us. We are God's children, and He takes care of those who believe. Our Father holds the power, and He is in control over every part of Creation. If we are wild women living out that wild way of faith and love, we will laugh at the days to come (Prov. 31:25) because Satan will be defeated like the pitiful thing that he is. God always gets the victory. We will be willing to do the task He is leading us to, and we will be ready to rise and stand firm.

If we really are free in Christ, filled with the power of the Holy Spirit, then we must live like the children of God that we are. We must not grow faint of heart, live in fear, or give into every one of life's woes and worries. We have a role to play, a task set before us, and we must not anticipate the next trial as a thing to run away from but an opportunity to rise up to.

When the people of Israel cried out to God for rescue, He sent Deborah (Judges 4-5). She awoke to the needs of the kingdom of God. She was an ordinary woman with great faith, a mother and homemaker who gave herself to the true power of prayer, and she arose to the task set before her. The people were suffering under the ruthless oppression of Sisera, an army commander of Canaan for twenty years. Deborah stirred the people to trust in God with an unwavering faith, and if the people returned to God, He would give them the victory over Sisera. They were strengthened in courage to fight. Deborah encouraged Barak to lead the people into battle, but his faith was small. He needed Deborah by his side, and together they gathered the troops. Although they were outnumbered, it says in Judges chapters 4 and 5 they arose as one: "Get ready! This is the day the Lord will give you victory over Sisera, for the Lord is marching ahead of you" (4:14 NLT). They were stirred in faith and marched forward together as one. Some stayed behind, safe on their property or settled by the seashore (5:16-18 NLT) and Deborah says these people of indecision who did not come to help the Lord are cursed (5:23 NLT). Do we want to be like the cowards of indecision or the courageous who arise? The ways of the Lord are wild, and He calls us to courage, as Deborah's song of prayer, "Lord, may all your enemies die like Sisera! But may those who love you rise like the sun in all its power!" (5:31 NLT). We weren't meant to sit home safely in the familiar. We are called to rise in faith.

Let's notice the bees for a minute. They are always buzzing in the background, producing honey or building comb, sometimes huddled in the hive on a rainy day, but never squandering the day. They are preparing to go back outside and forage or standing on guard to protect their liquid gold. They have a task to do and not a moment to waste—thousands of bees all playing their one small part to work unified as one mighty organism. They need a strong queen bee properly laying brood (baby bees) and caretaker bees surrounding her so she can do her job, along with the worker bees, the drones to fertilize the queen, the honey bees flapping their wings to evaporate the water out of the honey and the comb builders to cap the honey. There is nothing I can think of in all of Creation that portrays God's intricate design of the many parts working together as one body on one focused task. The goodness of God is always buzzing in the background wooing our heart, and when we slow down long enough to listen, we are reminded of the intricate ways He is working. He will grow our roots deep and prepare us for the task He has set before us, but we must listen and be willing to do what He asks us to do individually in the body of believers.

It may feel hard to be vulnerable to this new way of living in a community. It can be difficult to find safe people to open our hearts to, but God can pave the way. Practice talking with Him, be still before Him, and if there are still more areas of your heart that need healing, let a trusted friend come alongside you. Just as God waits with His arms wide open, there are dear people willing to hear your darkest parts and still love you. If you do not have that person in your life, ask God to bring you a friend who cares. She will stand out like a bright spot in a drab crowd. Listen to the still small voice nudging you to talk to her. You don't have to confess all your deepest secrets, but you can make a new friend. If that sounds scary to you, look for a warm-hearted person in your church. You are looking for the warm, sweet Spirit of the Lord, and when you see that person, you will know. She will radiate love and peace, eager to be your friend and pray with you. God's heart is for family to form and the body of believers to work together as one to move in His wild ways of loving one another.

We, as Christ-followers, should stand out like a city on a hill; our light shouldn't be hidden under a basket (Matt. 5:14 NLT). We are the salt that brings flavor to a tasteless world. Matthew teaches us that we are a lampstand that gives light to everyone in the household. We ought to be letting our light shine for all to see, so that everyone will praise our heavenly Father (Matt. 5:16 NLT). We are not boasting in our good deeds. We should be living out the special giftings He has given to each of us to display His glory. Paul teaches us in 1 Corinthians 1:4-11 that we are all given the areas of giftings that God has planted in us to blossom and be a blessing to others. God gives one person the special ability to give wise advice, another special knowledge, while another has great faith. He gives some the gift of healing or the power to perform miracles, while others the ability to prophesy. He gives someone else the ability to discern whether a message is from the Spirit of God or from another spirit. Still another person is given the ability to speak in unknown languages while another is given the ability to interpret what is being said. It is the one and only Spirit who distributes all these gifts (Romans 12 NLT). If you love being generous with your money, then generously bless the person on the side of the road—why don't you talk to her and hear her story while you're at it? You might just discover a new friend, or what a glorious day it would be if you could lead her to the Lord. If you love teaching, then go teach with the tenacity and enthusiasm of the Lord within you. If you can't hold back the notes in your soul from singing, then share the song with others and bee a blessing. If you have a word to share, then share out of the joy of your heart. We all have a part to play in the body of Christ (1 Cor. 12:27 NLT). We are responsible to obey and walk in our unique giftings wherever the Lord leads us, whether in the building of a church, a small home church in the backyard, or standing in line at the grocery store. If we are sitting stubborn, we are disobeying, and we are a dead part of the body.

We serve a wild God who isn't limited by any box or bank. If you have put your faith and hope in Him, then believe in all of Him; the God of the Bible who used a faithful homemaker to conquer Sisera, the God who healed the bleeding woman or told the lame man to pick up his mat and walk, the God who knew the heart of the Samaritan woman and showed great mercy. We serve that God, and that God can dwell in you if you believe.

Do you know the wild love of God?

Do you believe in the wild God of the Bible or just the parts that fit your cozy box?

Do you want to be a wild woman who learns to walk by faith in His wild ways?

What is your unique gifting and task God has called you to? If you're not sure, pray for God to reveal it to you.

### Action step #9.

Something may already be stirring in your heart. You know you are hesitating to step out—call that person, write a letter, show them you care or forgive them with genuine forgiveness. It doesn't have to be as drastic as marching into battle but if you are truly being prompted, it is time to obey. A wild woman in our upside-down world will simply "do the thing"

122

you know you should do. Sometimes just showing up is the wildest act of love and obedience.

# WILD WOMAN IS KNOWN BY
## *her fruit*

STEEPING TEA LEAVES IN WARM WATER
SOFTENS THE LEAVES AND RELEASES SWEET
AROMA AND FLAVOR. STEEPING IN GOD'S WORD
SOFTENS OUR HEART AND WE RADIATE HIS
SWEET SPIRIT, TENDER MERCY, AND WILD
LOVE.

WHAT STEP WILL YOU TAKE? WRITE IT OUT.
LUKE 6:43-46

Observation window and a sneak peek inside the hive.

# chapter 10

My sister was getting married, and I did not want to go to the wedding. Then mercy stepped in. Our relationship was as steady as shifting sands. We may have been two sisters who deeply loved each other but our steps were not in stride. We were on very different paths with expectations of the other that neither of us was meeting. There were seasons of silence, the chasm of emotional distance widened and I would slink back into the shadows where it seemed safe, letting the gaping wounds fester. I tried in my best intentions to throw out a lifeline only to be misunderstood as a pharisee pressing my own agenda. I couldn't see past my pain and the situation was a tangled ball of confusion. I couldn't make sense of it. During the year leading up to the wedding, there was no reconciliation, and the gaping hole had become so wide that there was no chance to catch my breath. The silence was deafening. I couldn't see past the wounds; I couldn't hear the truth, and I didn't want to go to a wedding when there was no peace. All I could do was leave the knot in God's hands and let Him untangle the mess.

It is beyond our comprehension how wide, how deep, how vast the Father's love is for us to cover those deep, wide wounds and heal them. Not only does He show His wild ways of sacrifice on the cross, but then He shows us there is even more. There's mercy. While Jesus was agonizing in his own pain and suffering, He lavished mercy on the people who put him there. "He has shown you, O mortal, what is good. And what does the Lord require of you? To act justly and to love mercy and to walk humbly with your God" (Micah 6:8 NLT). To follow the ways of Jesus is to love mercy even if we are still agonizing in our own pain. He didn't teach us to wait until relationships were perfect and healthy, so I've had to learn the hard way. I was agonizing in my own pain of unresolved hurts and wounds, and mercy said to set that pain aside, laying the pain at the cross and letting God work in His timing. I couldn't force my sister to break the silence and confront the wounds, and it seemed that was not going to happen in time for the big day.

A wedding season should be sweet months of planning and celebration, dresses and bridal showers, but my heart still had rotten roots of unforgiveness stealing my joy and the physical distance was feeding my affliction. Let me rewind back to the beginning where the weed of self-sins took root, not to dwell on it but to pluck it out. There was one year in elementary school I was being bullied every day and finding a new hiding spot at every recess. The girls would come to find me and throw rocks and sticks at me. They would circle around me and laugh. One day, a rock hit me in the head, and I started to bleed. I couldn't go back into class with blood dripping down my face, so I snuck past all the classroom windows, past the office, crouching in the bushes past the principal's office, and ran all the way home. My mom wasn't home, and I had to break a window to get into my room. I was hearing at Sunday school God had good plans for my life, but the girls at school were making my life miserable. My little mind was muddled on what the truth was. What was wrong with me? Why did the girls hate me? Where was God in the misery? Was this God's plan? Obviously I did not comprehend those words at that young age, but it was a message I was hearing and an inward battle I couldn't make sense of. Every day I came home after school crying—no one liked me. The seed of self-hatred was planted. I changed schools twice in the next two years, and sitting alone at the lunch tables gave room for the lies to take up residence. It was my tendency to turn inward and question why no one liked me. I was putting in all the effort and started to believe God must've made a mistake with me. The wounds of rejection were taking root, and the weed of self-pity was beginning to grow, overshadowing any light left in my young heart. I was fading to the background, believing no one noticed or understood me and learning it was safer to live in the shadows than to show any glimpse of who God made me to be. I had every opportunity given to me, and you wouldn't know it on the outside, but my school years became my cage. I felt like a bird with a broken wing, and I kept my wounds hidden.

It wasn't until the year before my sister's wedding that God's mercy led me into a quiet season to confront that deep root of self-pity and pluck it out. "Self-sins" is the love of self, self-ambition and jealousy. "For wherever there is jealousy and selfish ambition, there you will find disorder and evil of every kind" (James 3:16 NLT), any prideful sin that dwells on self and takes our focus away from the love of Jesus and loving others. It is self-seeking and spirals down into self-pity and despair, which can entrap us in a cage of depression. Self-pity found a way to the surface of my daily life in many seasons, but in this season, God was rooting it out, and it was brutally painful. The more I dwelled on myself and licked my own wounds, the more distracted I was from living my life, loving mercy and walking humbly with my God. We lose sight of Jesus and living our life according to His ways when we are focused on our own sins and sufferings. We will stay in that perpetual spin cycle when we face each day in our own strength, believing the lie "if I just try harder" we can keep going, only to fall at the second step of the day. The Lord does give new mercies every morning to face a new day but it is Satan who loves nothing more than to keep us in bondage to that mental cycle of despair. He wants to keep the key to our cage so we never break free of our bondage, and render us useless in the Kingdom of God. I lived in that bondage for a long time and gave the Enemy power over my thoughts. I believed I was doomed to a life of despair and accepted I would always struggle. The wedding weekend would have come and gone had I kept dwelling on myself. I was being tormented in my heart.

I was trying with all my best efforts to seek peace with my sister, so why was it such a shattered mess? We were trying to obey God in our choices and live according to His word so why did it seem so hard? Nothing made sense. The night terrors came back, and the cycle of suicidal thoughts was resurfacing. I couldn't escape the raging war inside. In His mercy, God prunes us, and He seems to use seasons of suffering when we're willing to surrender. If we're stubborn in one season, He will give us another opportunity. We don't want to surrender; we get stuck dwelling on the suffering but then we completely miss His mercy that brings us through seasons that will heal us and refine our faith. It's for our good. He doesn't want us to stay the same or live in the same darkness our whole lives. His heart is for us to be made new, to set us apart from the darkness and wickedness of the world. He didn't expect us to be perfect like He was in order to follow in His footsteps, but He does teach us to show mercy, care about the least of these, be willing to sell all we own to meet the needs, and consider others better than ourselves. Jesus teaches in the Sermon on the Mount the simplest truth, "Blessed are the merciful, for they will receive mercy" (Matt. 5:7 NLT). If we truly love mercy, we will love the whole Bible, not just the parts that our itching ears want to hear (2 Tim. 4:3-4 NLT), and we will learn to walk more sacrificially in the ways of Jesus.

But we live in tension between spirit and flesh. We rationalize and war, toiling in wounds or unresolved relationships. We can choose to follow Jesus and still be living with a wounded heart and a raging war in our soul. The turmoil can feel like a hurricane destroying every house in its path and snapping every tree in sight. Anger can rise until all we want to do is scream into a pillow or turn inward to numb the pain. Believing in Jesus and seeing the mercy He poured out does not mean we are instantly molded into perfection. It is the process of becoming free. We are sojourners, and the path is not easy, but God's mercy keeps pursuing us, His mercy keeps showing up. And every time we fall and choose mercy, we grow stronger and the light grows brighter. He sets us apart and sets us on a new path toward freedom. God gives us a free will to choose which step we will take in our suffering; and we can choose one of several choices. We can turn inward to our numbing vices ignoring the wounds we carry, we can busy ourselves to the point there is no time left for quiet, we can dwell on the problem draining our mental capacity, or we can choose to take the opportunity in suffering to be moldable and surrender to what the Lord is revealing. God is the Potter and we are the clay (Isaiah 64:8 NLT). He holds us in His hands, and we can allow Him to mold us how He sees and use us for the purposes He has in mind. We can look to Jesus and see He has a purpose to set free. The lies that form us don't have to hold us.

We live in a "no mercy" world telling us to live our one life to satisfy ourselves, but God's way is the opposite direction. His way is mercy. I was learning the hard way when I was desperately seeking to be noticed and looking to people to understand my pain or fill the void. In my desperation, I was attempting to get my sister to notice me, to be willing to work through the pain and resolve the issues. I was looking to her to be the balm of my wounds when only God is the Healer, and neither of us was showing any mercy or seeking to understand the other. When we live in the perpetual cycle of self, that cycle will continue to spin until mercy chooses to take a step in the opposite direction. God's way is for us to show mercy to others, and in choosing to do mercy, we receive mercy. "Blessed are the pure of heart for they will see God" (Matt. 5:8 NLT). He purifies our heart as we choose the way of mercy, and we are showered with blessing when we choose to set ourselves aside. It is a beautiful, incredible encounter with the Lord when we set our own pain aside and choose to show mercy to another. We can do it imperfectly but still choose to walk in His ways.

He shows us more of Himself and we are purified; we can see Him. That is God's plan. That was His plan all along to open our eyes to His great mercies.

I was pushing and pressuring to resolve the relationship in my own timing when my sister screamed at me to get to her wedding and hung up the phone. I sat there holding the dead phone completely stunned, and my thoughts were swirling— how could I possibly go now? I was not going to go. My mind was made up. My wounded heart was dictating my decision and clouding my view. She wasn't seeing me, and I couldn't make her see me. Any hope of reconciliation felt like a feather floating off in the wind, it felt useless. Instead of looking to God to fill my every need, I was looking to a person to validate my void. I said to my husband, "Even the craziest person on their worst day would not fly across the country to someone's wedding in these conditions." I sat quietly in the stillness of my outdoor garden room, staring out at the wide expanse of our property, at the end of my rope, and I heard a gentle voice say, "Obey and go."

God has so much more for you than you may comprehend. The ardor of God is to show mercy. He wants to meet your every need. He longs for you to see that. He waits for you to come to Him, and even when we don't, His mercy is always there, buzzing in the background and tenderly calling us to Himself like the sweet scent of honey drawing us to the hive. He says, "Don't let evil conquer you, but conquer evil by doing good" (Romans 12:21 NLT). God gently spoke to my heart in the stillness and said it was a matter of obedience to take that flight and go to that wedding. I had a peace that He would work things out in His timing. God's ways don't make sense in our rational minds; it is wild and goes against everything our own desires tell us to do. He not only asks us to love and consider others better than ourselves (Phil 2:3), but He also asks us to take a step further and show mercy. Weddings are supposed to be anticipated, and instead, I wanted to stay home. What should have been a season of joyful planning turned into angry phone calls ending abruptly. It made no rational sense to have any part of the day.

I have struggled with self-pity most of my life, living in the shadows, wanting to be noticed, and not fully realizing the sin. I was a wounded bird only dwelling on my own broken wing. That is the thing with self-sins. It's a perpetual inward cycle, and there is no way out until mercy steps in to stop the cycle. Self goes back onto self. If there is no instant gratification, we go back to what is "self" doing wrong. We fill that misery with more busyness, and it never satisfies. We wonder what we are doing wrong until we surrender to the way of Jesus and let him lead us out. I could have made my choice from bitterness and ignored the Lord's gentle guidance but I chose to lean into Him and learn from Him.

It takes work to break cycles and a willingness to surrender to the process. It takes faithfulness and persistence to steady on. We won't see the instant gratification or the immediate fruit in the work of breaking cycles. I was seeing more clearly that God's plan never had me at the center, but it was about me recognizing my place in His plan. It was His story all along to bring all people into a knowledge of His mercy. He points us to His fingerprints all over creation if we slow down long enough to notice and learn from Him. Those "self-sins" weren't magically corrected after one step of obedience to attend a wedding. God, in His mercy, was untangling all the lies I had come to believe, and the work wasn't finished. He was about to stretch me further and prune me deeper to reveal the root problem. We all want to be noticed—we were made to love and be loved, to know and be known. We desperately want that and seek to fulfill that longing in relationships. We search in all the wrong places until we encounter the love of God the Father and grasp His deep love for us in the true gospel of Jesus.

Satan is the god of this world, blinding the minds of those who don't believe. They are unable to see the glorious light of the Good News (2 Cor. 4:3 NLT). Satan is working to confuse our minds, keep us in bondage and distract us from seeing the love of God. He wants us to stay trapped in our pride and mark us useless. The ways of this world are to deceive us and sweep us into the stream of satisfying the self. We can choose to stay in that stream our whole life. God's way is the other direction, upstream, and away from ourselves. We don't have to accept our selfishness and identify with our sin. There is a way to unlatch that door and fly free: love mercy and walk humbly with God. Choose the way of mercy and listen to His voice in the stillness.

I battle with this chapter because I'm not a wonderfully completed masterpiece who has become the perfect example of mercy, but I can share with you how God continues to teach me. Jesus said, "I tell you the truth, unless you turn from your sins and become like little children, you will never get into the kingdom of heaven. So anyone who becomes as humble as this child is the greatest in the Kingdom of Heaven." (Matt.18:2-4 NLT). Jesus' teachings are always the simple truth. I have been humbled and brought to the quiet place of prayer many times, where I see the simple choice in front me to change or continue to be tossed on the spin cycle. It takes persistence in prayer to break off certain patterns and defeat lies.

Children have their little sin natures, but they are pure of heart with a simplicity of faith. They don't battle with accumulated wounds or analyze life's great mysteries. They simply forgive and get back to playing.

Rex B. Andrews in "What the Bible Teaches About Mercy" says, "It takes, at times mayhap, persistence. But the turning to God, and the thinking of His good thoughts, robs the evil spirit of its power. And the answer to the prayer destroys the evil. What happens when you pray such a prayer in the case of these evil things? The angels come forth and separate the evil from the good. The Holy Spirit defeats and casts down the unclean spirit and all its lusts. For all lusts of evil are opposite to the true love of lowliness and mercy. The will of God is mercy, which means to give, to fill the need. The whole kingdom of God goes into action, and into motion to accomplish that mercy and to fill the need when the believer prays. True lowliness prays so, and TRIUMPHS, for the Holy Spirit is the Spirit of prayer. And the lowliness is the Holy Spirit. And the mercy is the ardor of the Holy Spirit to do good."

The whole kingdom of God goes into action when the believer prays. Imagine that. When we love our lust and dwell on our own self and sufferings, we hate mercy. When we choose mercy and pray, the whole kingdom of God goes into action. If we accept we are just going to be sinners, suffering our whole lives, we are blatantly denying scripture and the power we have through the Holy Spirit to conquer the sin. Isn't that good news? We don't have to trudge through life waiting for Jesus. We can be more than conquerors in Christ (Rom. 8:37 NLT). But we can't love God and live in the darkness. The true gospel has the power to transform lives so we don't have to live a lukewarm existence. The will of God is true love of lowliness and mercy. That's the simple gospel. That day in the garden room, I had a choice to live in my dark pit and dwell on self or love God and book the plane ticket.

If we all became more like children in our faith, loving the way of mercy, there would be an abundance of fruit falling off our branches. There would be less orphans without a home and more widows would be welcomed into families; churches would be bursting to the brim with believers who deeply grasp the deep, wide, vast love of the Father. If we looked to the Bible to learn what God glories in, we would see He loves mercy, and we would be His hands and feet of mercy.

Jesus became lowly and loved others. He noticed the leper, and when everyone was scared to get within six feet of him, Jesus was right there, laying hands on him and healing him (Matt. 8:1-4 NLT). He noticed Zaccheus up in the tree and said He was coming to his house for dinner (Luke 19:1-10 NLT). He noticed the blind man longing to see and restored his sight (John 9 NLT). God has humbled me and pruned away many branches until I had nothing left but Him. I'm still a fortunate American, blessed with family and food on my table so I can't claim poverty or despair, but I have seen the poverty of my spirit and my great need for a Savior. I have seen my depravity and the selfishness I am capable of pursuing. I know the darkness of being separated from my Savior when I have chosen to curl up in my ball of self-pity and lock myself behind doors. In those deepest, darkest places, I saw God's mercy on me.

Paul tells us in Galatians the result of following our own selfish desires. He teaches us that we are constantly fighting the two forces within ourselves to follow the sinful nature or to walk in the Spirit. When we choose our selfish nature, it leads to decay and many sins such as sexual immorality, impurity, lustful pleasures, idolatry, sorcery, hostility, quarreling, jealousy, outbursts of anger, selfish ambition, dissension, division, envy, drunkenness, wild parties, and other sins like these. He says anyone living that sort of life will not inherit the Kingdom of God (Galatians 5:19-21 NLT).

I include the whole list because we all fit into that list somewhere, but if we choose to settle in and get comfortable living in the darkness of any one of those sins, we will not inherit the kingdom of God. A life of darkness and living for ourselves leads to decay. The Holy Spirit convicts our heart and reveals our sin so we will repent and turn away from that sin. He wants to change us and transform our hearts, bringing us life and growth. The beauty of the gospel is the mercy He shows to give us chance after chance to turn away from any sin and to be a sheep who follows His voice. He left the ninety-nine sheep to go after the one lost sheep (Luke 15 NLT). He left the crowd to go after you.

I have shared stories with many of those sins weaved throughout and recognized the impact self-sins have on the way I choose to live each day. God, in His mercy, has shown me I have the choice every moment of every day to follow my selfish desire, or I can choose to go against that and choose the way of mercy. It is not an easy choice. Sometimes it's like swimming upstream in white waters, other times, we just don't want to choose it. We would rather cozy up and numb our minds. Mercy goes against everything our "self" wants to do. We don't want to be the first one to go to our spouse and apologize. We don't want to ask our children to forgive us for our angry reaction. I certainly did not want to fly across the country to attend a family wedding. When the bitter weed has choked out any light from entering, we don't want to walk in mercy. We want to stay in our selfish cycle of despair and wallow in our self-pity. The lust of our heart takes control, and it is much easier to let time tick by and emotional distance to widen. I went to the wedding, and it was a moment-to-moment choice surrendering my heart to God's ways. I had to step into the hallways to let runaway tears escape, but then God was my strength to walk back in. I left my wounds outside while He showed up to the party. I came home from that wedding and continued to wrestle through my own weeds. God was still working in my heart and He revealed the deepest root issue all along was bitterness and unforgiveness.

It was deep self-hatred rooting back to the schoolyard that grew over time and festered in the shadows. I had allowed wounds to accumulate, but Satan used the distance between sisters both physically and emotionally to strangle me. Time continued to pass by, and there was no change, no word, just crickets; she was in the newlywed season, and I had to leave any unresolved issues in God's hands. The silence was unbearable. The silence deepened my wounds. There seemed to be no glimmer of hope and bitterness had a chokehold.

I started to see not only had God been healing my broken wing, but He needed time to work on hers too and I had to trust God's ways are much higher than my ways. Even if the wounds were still there, that was okay. I was allowed to feel wounded, but I was not allowed to live in the wounds. I could see God's heart is to heal as we choose to lean into Him. He showed me mercy was the only way out of the swirling. I knew I had to break the silence. I picked up the phone to call my sister, asking for forgiveness for my wrongs. There was no answer. I had a heart pounding split-second decision to leave a message or hang up. Voicemail beeped and words started bubbling out, words of genuine repentance that was no longer about validating myself or filling my bottomless void but about honoring God. I hung up the phone, and for the first time in years, I felt peace. I was right with God. I found true freedom in following the way of Jesus and seeking forgiveness. I had no expectations of her calling back, maybe ever, so when I saw her name calling later that day, I yelled to the whole house it was a miracle. She thanked me for the message, and we had a beautiful conversation. It didn't magically morph into a perfect, healthy sister relationship right then, but it felt like a fresh start. God set me on a new path to hear His voice and direction even if the relationship never grew in the ways I had hoped. I knew I had to be right with God and obey Him in doing my part.

We are freed from the lusts of our hearts and the heavy yoke of bondage when we choose to show mercy and walk in the light as Jesus is in the light. When we have a heart of mercy, the darkness flees, and we are the ones who are changed even if the other person chooses to go their own way. We do our part and leave the rest in God's hands. He sets us free, and our hearts are right with Him. He satisfies our deepest longing to be noticed and lights the way out of the pit. When we choose to glory and revel in the things God glories in, we are honoring Him. We find contentment when we look to Him to fill our every need. It's in the process as we take steps of obedience that we are set free. He grows the ardor, the passion to be holy as He is holy, and little by little, that pain no longer has power over us. Choosing mercy destroys the temptation to dwell on self. Light comes in and destroys all darkness.

Jesus is the guiding light out of our sin and darkness (John 8:12 NLT). As we walk in the light, God will continue to grow the light brighter and brighter until the glorious day when Jesus will be revealed, and every knee will bow and every tongue will confess, He is Lord (Philippians 2:10-11 NLT). We are to be those willing vessels to do mercy in a dark world— sharing the Light of Jesus with others or the darkness will continue to cave in all around us. People living with no hope will continue to live in their despair if we choose to let darkness consume our minds and paralyze us from truly living. When we know the truth and are set free, we are responsible to live in that truth and show that same mercy to others that God has shown us. We can give that same hope and freedom to others He has given us.

It is God's heart for all people to come to Him, no matter how dark the cloud, how deep the despair, or hopeless the night. He says "Come." We can come boldly to the throne of our gracious God, and there we will receive mercy and find grace to help us when we need it most (Heb. 4:16 NLT). When we come to His throne boldly and humble ourselves, we are walking in the light and learning from the lowliness of Jesus. The pure will know God, show mercy, and see God. The more we choose to walk humbly with our Lord, the more we are changed like little children, and the light will shine brighter. That is God's glorious plan of revealing Jesus: as the light grows brighter, the darkness flees. Are you seeing it?

We are to be the ones that shine brighter and brighter. "Your love for one another will prove to the world that you are my disciples" (John 13:35

NLT). That is the wonder we see in the blooming, flowering, fruiting of mercy all throughout Scripture: the mercy of Jesus. He left us with the task to be torchbearers, and we are the ones to show that love and mercy. When I saw this truth was always buzzing in the background of every part of my life, weaving through every part of Scripture, it was a moment of brokenness and humility seeing myself for who I really am. It was all God's mercy working on my heart in every season so I could see Him and forgive others the way He forgave me. He wanted me to see Him all along. He wanted me to stop and notice the bees humming a merry song in the background.

All along He had you in mind, and when we step back and see the design in the grander tapestry, we can't help but sing praises and savor the sweet honey He gives us each day to enjoy. It's not in our strength and effort, but it is reveling in His goodness. We were made to praise Him with all our heart (Psalm 19) and be like the children singing "Jesus Loves Me." He will continue to capture our whole heart until Jesus returns, but until that day, we are to be ready and right with Him.

Is your heart right with the Lord?

Do you want to see God?

Who can you forgive and show mercy to today?

**Action step #10.**

Time to pick up the phone and seek forgiveness or write that letter of apology. Go boldly to the throne room, to your quiet place of prayer and pour out the toxic emotions in your notebook. If the letter is still laced with angry bitterness, write a fire letter and burn it, then quiet your heart with the Lord before you write a letter of mercy. "Be still and know that I am God! I will be honored by every nation. I will be honored throughout the world" (Psalm 46:10 NLT). He will work in your heart and burn away the dross as you sit in stillness with Him. It is a choice to surrender. It is a choice to show mercy, but it frees you from the toxins eroding away at your heart and thoughts.

# "ACT JUSTLY
## LOVE MERCY
### WALK HUMBLY
### WITH YOUR GOD."
#### MICAH 6:8

AM I EAGER TO SHOW MERCY
AND BE RIGHT WITH GOD?
LOOK UP THE DEFINITION OF
"ARDOR":

GOD FEELS THAT WAY ABOUT YOU, AND WHEN
WE REALIZE THAT, WE WANT TO SHOW THE
SAME MERCY TO OTHERS.

Some of our first honey harvest. These frames can weigh upward to 14 pounds when fully capped.

# chapter 11

Those self-sins were not magically corrected with one trip across the country to the wedding. It took persistence and bold prayers over that next year before I could see the unforgiveness in my heart and make that phone call.

The home church of families had sprouted, and our true struggles were starting to surface—the weary souls, the pain, the broken and bruised–but there was so much growth and life, too. I was still wrestling with the tendency of looking to people for affirmation, but God was steadfast and slow to teach this time. That step of obedience to go to the wedding tilled my heart, making me more ready to receive all that God was revealing. He was changing me and truly transforming me, maybe for the first time. The squabbles still existed among believers, but God was working in His mysterious, wild ways.

At the turn of the new year, 2023, I was compelled to do a fast and found myself in the middle of some kind of fierce battle. God was giving me insight into the true heart condition of His people, He gave me a glimpse into the spiritual realm, and I was terrified of what I saw. I was crying out to Him to hide us safe beneath the shelter of His wing (Psalm 61:4 NLT). We desperately needed Him to draw near to us and astonish us, knowing He is the God of restoration and redemption. We were drowning in our selfishness and pride, the baggage we carried, and the accumulated wounds that were never confronted. All I knew to do was run to God and surrender in prayer and fasting.

The storm in my soul rolled in, the dark clouds settled in, and the thunder was booming. The torment in my mind was raging, and thoughts were firing from every direction. The swirling hurricane in my heart had erupted, and all I could do was run. Everything in me was screaming to run as far away as I could. I hadn't eaten for days, my head was pulsing in pain, but I was compelled to run. The ardor, the deep painful desire, the fury, the hungry passion to see God move and answer prayers I had boldly prayed compelled me to run on an empty stomach and not to stop until I got to the end of the road. All along the way, the Lord was speaking to me. The dead carcass on the side of the road, the abandoned house, the tree uprooted from a storm, the memorial cross of a son who had passed, a mailbox with the words "The New Eden" weathered and worn; all reminders of the depravity of this decaying world. The anger in my soul was rising, the righteous anger to fight on my knees in prayer.

When we are worn down to our very last ounce of energy, all we have left is fighting on our knees in prayer. The emptiness in the pit of my stomach was rumbling like a ravenous wild beast. I was hungry, but I was desperate to know more of God and to break down the plans the Enemy had to destroy God's people. The fury in my soul was rising, and it was time to go back home. I felt defeated and I was crumbling under the attack. My spirit was fighting, but my flesh was weak. I got home and opened the refrigerator, ready to warm up the creamy, cheesy macaroni and give up on the fast. I stared into the bowl so broken, so ready to quit, and in my weakest moment, my fear of the Lord was stronger. I put the lid back on and locked myself in my room to pray and cry out to God. I needed to hear from God. I needed a breakthrough.

Be warned! I am about to describe a raging war that was happening behind that door. The spiritual war in the unseen is very real and when we are fasting, we are standing in the gap of prayer while God is working. Daniel was called to a fast, and it took twenty-one days for the angel, Michael, to get through the spiritual battle (Daniel 10). Satan sent me into a tailspin of spiraling thoughts. I was seeing something like demons, it sounded like screaming bats around my head, and I felt paralyzed. It got very dark, and my husband started knocking on the door, but I couldn't move. He kept knocking and I could hear him getting concerned but I was stuck, curled up in my ball. He had to break down the door. I am ashamed to admit I was kicking at him to get out, all I kept saying was "they're screaming, the bats are screaming." I realize that sounds intense, but it was like I was overcome by this dark battle. He finally got his arms around me and held me, and then I saw a break of light and a hand reaching down saying, "Take my hand, come to Me." That day was a breaking point, day seventeen of the fast, and the heavy darkness inside lifted and lost its power over me. That day planted a seed of boldness in my soul to share the truth of the gospel and served as a daily reminder to honor God. We are not to look to man for our fulfillment and affirmation. Only God fills our every need.

"I prayed to the Lord, and he answered me. He freed me from all my fears. Those who look to him for help will be radiant with joy, no shadow of shame will darken their faces" (Psalm 34:4-5). That day set into motion a new fervor to obey what God was laying on my heart to share and to share with boldness. The spirit of fear and timidity was broken, and a renewed sense of urgency was simmering. "In my desperation I prayed, and the Lord listened; he saved me from all my troubles. For the angel of the Lord is a guard; he surrounds and defends all who fear him" (Ps.34:6-7 NLT). I was paralyzed and desperate—the fast was cracking me wide open and revealing the rot. I couldn't help but share what the Lord was doing! "Taste and see that the Lord is good. Oh! The joys of those who take refuge in Him" (Psalm 34:8 NLT). We are to fear Him and walk in boldness, not fearing what man thinks. We live to please an audience of One.

Jesus fasted for forty days and nights, he was hungry, and then the Spirit led Him into the desert to be tempted by Satan. In the gospel of Matthew, he tells how Jesus was tempted three times. He had already been worn down; for forty days, he had eaten nothing. He was suffering for the sake of the gospel in preparation for the ministry the Father had for Him in advance. Jesus had perfect, unwavering faith, and He was never tempted to quit. After Satan's three attempts to make him fall, Jesus never faltered and Satan went away. "Satan went away, and angels came and took care of Jesus" (Matt. 3:11 NLT). There is an end to the battle, relief from the swirling storm. When we pray bold prayers, we must be ready for the storms to come.

Our storms will look different, but as we learn from Jesus and push through those painful, testing moments and persevere to the end, we will see the battle relent and angels come to us. We will suffer for Christ as we obey His leading, but knowing we are right where He wants us means we can have joy. When we choose security in Christ over comfort of culture, we are doing the will of the Father. All throughout the Bible, God led men and women through fires and suffering for His name's sake. In our obedience, we are called into suffering for His name's sake. Daniel faithfully and consistently loved the Lord with all his heart. He didn't give Him small parts or choose when to give; he loved God with his whole heart. He was firmly planted in the knowledge of God, and when the trials came, he was pleasing an audience of One. He stayed faithful and persisted in prayer every day. When his devotion to God led him into the lion's den, his faith was deeply rooted, and he was ready for it.

This was just another trial to endure, and if it took his life, it didn't matter. He was going to be faithful to God no matter where the path led him. All throughout the Bible, we see that God is after our whole heart. He is after our heart to be bold and courageous so others will see His mighty works and that His glory can be on display. It is for the purpose of bringing all people into a knowledge of who He is and be drawn into His presence. It is so we will pray bold prayers, and as we pray boldly, He will strengthen us. I read about Daniel's life, and it strengthens me; it stirs my heart to stay the course. "We can rejoice, too, when we run into problems and trials, for we know that they help us develop endurance. And endurance develops strength of character, and character strengthens our confident hope of salvation. And this hope will not lead to disappointment. For we know how dearly God loves us, because he has given us the Holy Spirit to fill our hearts with his love" (Romans 5:3-5 NLT).

Trials are an expected part of walking on a broken path. We will come up to rocks in the road, cracks to jump over, walls to climb. It is all meant to strengthen us in our fervor to stay faithful. Trials will come whether we are following God's voice or not. Trials are the result of a sinful world. We are going to get tangled up and deceived. We are going to veer off the path and follow the twists and turns if we are only relying on our own strength and logic. We have that choice. We can go our own way all day, every day until our last day. But if you're not satisfied with that kind of life and you're ready to pray bold prayers, then gird yourself up. Those trials will come. They are meant to strengthen you, and they may lead you to suffering and fires, but there is a purpose in every moment of the swirling in your soul. God hasn't changed, becoming cruel or inflicting pain without purpose—He is present in our pain. "Though he brings grief, he also shows compassion because of the greatness of his unfailing love. For he does not enjoy hurting people or causing them sorrow." (Lam. 3:32-33 NLT).

God allows those trials and temptations to test your faith. God allowed Satan to test Jesus in the desert at the end of his fast when his flesh was worn down. There was a purpose in the moment, and though Jesus was perfect and sinless, not tempted by Satan's taunting, He was still faced with the choice to eat or not to eat, to jump or not to jump, to take authority over all the kingdoms or not to, and though He wasn't going to give in, He was modeling for us the power we have over Satan. We can swat him away and grab hold of the hand of God. Jesus just swats Satan away like a pesky fly buzzing in His ear. He says, "Get out of here Satan" (Matt. 4:10 NLT), and the next verse says the angels immediately came to him. I was faced with the choice in my hunger to eat the cheesy noodles or choose God. In the moment, we have a choice. In my moment of weakness, I may have put the noodles back, but the battle raged on. There was a new resolve to continue the fight in fasting and persevere to the end, believing in the answers to prayer I couldn't see just yet and trusting God was still working.

Amy Carmichael says, "Faith doesn't ask why... Faith just trusts."

When God brought us to the farm, faith wasn't asking why. Faith wasn't questioning the reason for the trials. Faith wasn't complaining about the painful pruning we were going through. The pruning away and the pain I was experiencing in the deepest parts of my soul were for a purpose. It was growing the spiritual fruit of faithfulness and long-suffering. Faith doesn't see what God is doing when He puts on the gloves and pulls out the pruning shears. We can scream for Him to stop and put that scary sharp object away, but because He loves us so deeply and knows what is best for us, He isn't going to inflict pain on purpose. He allows the pain to be used for a purpose. He knows the fruit produced down the road. Of course, He won't force us to let Him. He is never forceful or mean. He is a patient, purposeful Gardener, but when we relent and rest, His gentle hands come in and start the work. Faith cannot see the fruit at the end of the season. Faith just trusts He is working. When it is His perfect timing, He lets the fruit emerge in all its glory.

We are being built up and strengthened day by day. He is restoring us, untangling the lies Satan tries to use to entangle us. He is bringing us back onto a path that leads to holiness and righteousness, and that path is not comfortable. It is not for the faint of heart, those unwilling to move forward or do the work. That is a path that requires unwavering faith, a yearning to pray bold prayers, and a willingness to do the work and obey God's leading. Matthew teaches us to effectively pray, "Keep on asking, and you will receive what you ask for. Keep on seeking, and you will find. Keep on knocking, and the door will be opened to you" (Matt. 7:7 NLT). He goes on to use the example of a child asking his parents for a loaf of bread. They don't give him a stone to eat. If the child wants some fish, they don't give him a snake. Parents want good things for their children. God wants so much more for us than we can comprehend, but we have to learn to trust Him. We grow in our boldness the more trust builds. We learn true happiness is trusting our Heavenly Father and obeying what He is asking us to do. The path He leads us on is not the easy path. Paul can tell you the path he walked on after he put his trust and faith in God was far from the easy path. Paul's path led him into towns that rejected him, mocked him, put him in prison, tortured him and eventually killed him. Daniel's path led him into a lion's den.

The path that leads to life is narrow. The Bible says in Matthew 7:13 (NLT), "You can enter God's Kingdom only through the narrow gate. The highway to hell is broad, and its gate is wide for the many who choose that way. But the gateway to life is very narrow and the road is difficult, and only few ever find it." That verse always terrified me, but it isn't meant to scare us. God, in His mercy, is always drawing us to Himself, always weaving beauty into the background until we slow down and notice that He has been there the whole time, gently calling our name and asking us to put our faith in Him. He is inviting us to drop our burdens and follow Him. Jesus didn't paint a pretty picture for his disciples when He said, "If any of you wants to be my follower, you must turn from your selfish ways, take up your cross, and follow me. If you try to hang on to your life, you will lose it. But if you give up your life for my sake, you will save it." (Matt. 16:24-25 NLT).

This life was never intended to stay in the security of your home, nestled in the safety of a comfortable church and storing up treasures. If we want to turn from our selfish ways and go where God leads us, that is where we find freedom and life abundant. The disciples left behind successful businesses, some left their families, and one left his wife at home to go walk with Jesus. Jesus walked the earth and modeled his ministry to his followers for three years, but those followers had to give up their comforts. They had to leave everything behind, not knowing where they would go, if there would be food to eat or clothes to wear; they were just asked to have faith and trust in their Lord. Jesus warns, "If you try to hang on to your life, you will lose it. But if you give up your life for my sake, you will save it. What benefits do you have if you gain the whole world but lose your soul? Is anything worth more than your soul?" (Matt. 16:25-26 NLT).

Is that addiction so satisfying that you're willing to lose your soul over it? Is that temptation worth it? Are you knowingly living in sin and choosing to believe it is okay for you to do? The true disciples, the twelve chosen Apostles of Jesus, didn't make excuses for their sins or choose to stay at home where it was safe. Jesus was speaking to those who were serious about their faith. They were bold, ready, and willing to follow Jesus wherever He was going to lead. Are you a follower serious about your faith? The disciples turned from their selfish ways, and they followed Him.

These twelve Apostles spent three profoundly impactful years with Jesus, being discipled by Him and growing to love Him with all their hearts. After the ascension of Jesus, they all scattered and went on to spread the Good News of the gospel, making disciples to all parts of the world. They walked out their faith in boldness and courage, willing to die if that moment came, and many of them did lose their life for their faith. They were clubbed and stabbed to death, crucified upside down, brutally beaten with rods and stoned, and beheaded. Ten were martyred, one died of old age, and one turned his gaze inward and ended his own life. Are we serious about our faith to the point of death?

The path to eternal life is not a comfortable life. If you feel the hurricane in your heart will never calm or hope for your weary soul is nowhere in sight, it may feel that way in this moment. But rest and hope is right there within reach. The comfort of Jesus is only a whisper away. You can choose to turn your eyes to Him and accept His grace and forgiveness, no matter how broken and bruised you are. That anger, those wounds or scars in your heart may still be there. You can scream at the top of your lungs, you can sob until your eyes are puffy, you can even have days when the pain inside is agonizing, but Jesus is still there. He never said that pain would disappear in a magical moment. You can always come back to the cross where you first saw the light and found rest. I have been curled up in a fetal position crying on the floor, not wanting to go on or face another day, and then my loving Father reaches out His hand and reminds me gently to persevere. Many times, He uses people to show us His mercy in physical form. My two-year-old daughter quietly climbed onto my lap, tenderly held my face in her little hands, and wiped away my tears before laying her head on my chest. If Jesus walked in the room and saw me there, that is what He would do. He wants to lift us out of our pit, out of the mire, and walk with us in marvelous light. Isaiah had a word from the Lord when he was talking to the Israelites about freedom from Babylon: "This is what the Lord says—your Redeemer, the Holy One of Israel: I am the Lord your God, who teaches you what is good for you and leads you along the paths you should follow. Oh, that you had listened to my commands! Then you would have had peace flowing like a gentle river and righteousness rolling over you like waves in the sea" (Isaiah 48:17-18 NLT). The Lord wants that freedom for us today, to follow the path that is good for us and listen to His commands as we trust Him and walk in boldness. Then His peace will flow like a gentle river and His righteousness will roll over us like waves in the sea.

I have bruises in my heart that aren't fully healed, but I can still choose to let the loving hands of my Father restore those dark spots, and little by little, He will do that. As I was reminded on my run of fury, we live in a decaying world. The once-beautiful garden sign that read "The New Eden" that is now weathered and rusted was on display as a reminder of this deteriorating world. We are but a vapor. The bruises will fade, the brokenness will heal, and none of this pain will last. "The grass withers and the flowers fade, but the word of our God stands forever" (Isaiah 40:8 NLT). Let's be women who live with an eternal focus, listening to His commands and walking out our faith in boldness. We live to please an audience of One.

How is the boldness in your soul building up?

Are you willing to say, "Wherever you lead Lord I will go"?

Are you willing to lose friends or family, lose your dream house, even lose your life for your faith?

**Action step #11.**

 Bold step here—are you ready for it? You have a gift in your soul to share with others, a passion that needs to be shared, an inspired idea, a ministry to start, a group to lead or a new path to pave. It may be time to come out of hiding and send your wild heart into the world. We are co-creators with the God of the universe, and He has given you giftings to create beauty in the world; a word of encouragement, wisdom or knowledge, a writing or a song. Sometimes God puts those giftings up high on a shelf so we can have time to grow and be more ready when we grab hold. Your beauty and femininity was never meant to be hidden. "In the same way, let your good deeds shine out for all to see, so that everyone will praise your heavenly Father" (Matt.5:16 NLT) Bee bold. Be strong. The Lord will be with you.

# "Charm is deceptive,

## BEAUTY DOES NOT LAST BUT A WOMAN WHO FEARS THE LORD IS TO BE PRAISED."
## PROVERBS 31:30 NLT

## WALK IN BOLDNESS
## WHERE IS THE LORD LEADING YOU?

# chapter 12

I noticed a woodpecker on the way back from my run of fury. We can usually hear woodpeckers off in the distance and not think much of it, but this guy was right there in front of me. I just stood there, mesmerized by the moment. Maybe I was too exhausted to run any farther, but I was fully present and listening. I was quietly watching the woodpecker and heard God's still, small voice saying I was like that woodpecker, pecking at the walls of my sister's heart and hurting people with my relentless pushing. In a sudden swirl of connecting dots, I realized I was the woodpecker; even with the best intentions to get deep inside to the rot killing our relationship, I was pushing my sister too hard. That was the moment I saw the deepest root of my bitterness and unforgiveness. I was the problem, and I had to change. I was expecting her to be the one to change, blaming her for my wounds and carrying a bitterness that was paralyzing me. Woodpeckers peck at the toughest bark to get deep inside at the bugs that will kill a tree from the inside out. It requires a powerful peck to get to the cause of the rot. God had been gently knocking at the doors of my heart to show me the unforgiveness I was harboring for my sister and the intensity of my actions. Jesus is gentle and I was not being gentle or kind.

All I could do was thank Him for showing me the truth of my own rot. *Thank you, Lord, for what You have done. Thank you, Lord, for the work you are doing.*

God sees you. Thank the Lord, for His mercy endures forever! "The heavens proclaim the glory of God. The skies display his craftsmanship. Day after day they continue to speak; night after night they make him known" (Psalm 19:1-2 NLT). Thanking the Lord in our struggle feels strange. That moment came after a step of obedience to fly to the wedding, after a year of persistence in prayer, after difficult days in a fast and that was the same day I had the battle behind doors. It was a heart of thanksgiving starting to emerge out of that journey of faith.

Thanking the Lord for a wound we carry feels unnatural. Who wants to thank Him when we have been hurt or are deep in a hole of suffering? We want the person who hurts us to feel our pain, to know they hurt us. We want them to notice we are in pain, so we spew words out of our own pain. We may seek attention and validation. Thanking the Lord goes against everything we want to do. We don't want to thank Him for a trial we are going through, certainly not for suffering. We are too stuck in our head to see past our pain. It feels like a foggy cloud in our minds, blocking any clarity. It hinders us from functioning day to day. We can choose to muster up the strength to say "Thank you, Lord, for whatever this thorn is," but we may not feel thankful in the moment. We can say, "I don't know why it is so confusing right now or why it hurts so deeply, but I still trust You." If we choose to keep our mouths shut, too stubborn to say, "Thank you, God, for the work You are doing," it is only hurting us. It allows the bitter weed to take over and our hearts to grow darker. Satan wins. He loves it when we are self-focused and introspective in our own thoughts and feelings. It keeps us living under the foggy cloud. When we are praising the Lord, the wound may still be there, but the foggy cloud will lift. Praise is our strongest weapon. Thankfulness drowns out the enemy.

I often want to pound on the walls, peck on the bark like a woodpecker, until I get through to the reward. I can come across as fiery and intense, and all my life, I saw that as my "broken wing," a part of myself where I was convinced God must have made a mistake. When a woodpecker has a wound, they have to hobble around in the wilderness to heal. They are forced to be resourceful and build their strength back up to fly, but then they develop the stamina to peck through the toughest of trees. They can teach us to look beneath the surface and find the bravery within ourselves to let those walls and barriers come down. There is always more to us under the surface, more behind that wall, more behind the mask. We just have to be willing to dig deeper and be vulnerable. It takes courage to know and be known.

When God began the work of healing in my heart, He showed me that what I thought was a "broken wing" was a personality trait He intentionally chose to give me for my good and to shine for His glory. When that intense passion to pound down the wall is used in my own selfish way and timing, it hurts people and scares people off. That trait inflicted wounds in the sister relationship and I couldn't fix it. All I could do was repent and ask her forgiveness. When I yield the personality trait under God's care and mercy, He can use it to bring walls down and let the beauty burst out in His much gentler way. I giggle here thinking of the scene in Beauty and the Beast where Beast pounds on the door, demanding Belle to come down to dinner. He has to be reminded to ask her gently, and of course, in his boiling rage, he can't control his angry outburst. She is even more stubborn to stay in her room. We can pound on people and pester and nag, but if they are not ready to share or let their guard down, that is when Jesus gently reminds us to back off and yield to His ways. My stubborn heart needed a lot of correcting, but like a woodpecker determined to get to her beetle dinner she can hear scampering around inside the tree, I am determined to get past that wall and allow God to get to the rot.

In God's ardor to meet my needs and heal my broken parts, He so gently reminds me of compassion for others who also need time to heal. We all have areas of brokenness and "broken wings." Some women are more like sparrows minding their own business, loyal and quiet in the background; some are like hummingbirds buzzing in and out, shining in the sun; while others are like parakeets, happy to be home. The thing with birds is they are not truly happy being caged in, even if they are home birds, and the essence of what they are can't be lived out when they have a broken wing. But birds are resilient. They are capable of healing and flying once again. I believe God created birds for so many reasons—to show He cares for the birds of the air but also to teach us His heart for His daughters. He longs for us to be healed and whole, flying free and happy. One day we will be. But while we have breath, He wants us to look to the birds (Matt. 6:26 NLT). He takes care of them and feeds them. He notices and watches over the sparrows. "God cares so wonderfully for wildflowers that are here today and thrown into the fire tomorrow, He will certainly care for you. Why do you have so little faith?" (Matt. 6:30 NLT). He wants to get deep inside to the rot. He cares that you find healing, and as we yield to His process of healing, we thank Him.

We begin to say, "Thank you, Jesus. Thank you Lord," over and over, even if we don't feel like it. You can grit it between your teeth. It will start to break the foggy cloud. I sing the hymn "I Need Thee Every Hour" some days through torment and tears, and when the heaviness lifts, I sing it as praise. The Lord sees our heart and what we need. He can meet us in that need and give us exactly what we are longing for; a song comes on the radio, a verse in the Bible jumps off the page, a friend calls at the right moment, our toddler crawls up on our lap and strokes our face. He is a creative God who takes notice of every detail of our messy, complicated hearts, and He knows just what we need. We, as women, can let that broken wing set, and we can learn to live with it. It can become a part of who we are and believe there is no hope for healing. The Lord comes to the broken-hearted, and we can start thanking Him, brokenness and all. We can thank Him for the wounds.

And one day, we will all be completely healed and restored, flying free in glory. That is something we can thank and praise the Lord for no matter what wounds we still carry or brokenness we still feel. Imagine a sweet friend or mentor who brings you comfort. Paul, in his gentle, wise comfort, sits Timothy down and encourages him. "Timothy, you certainly know what I teach, and how I live, and what my purpose in life is. You know my faith, my patience, my love, and my endurance. You know how much persecution and suffering I have endured. You know all about how I was persecuted in Antioch, Iconium, and Lystra, but the Lord rescued me from it all" (2 Tim. 3:10-11 NLT). But the Lord rescued him. He wasn't crippled in pain or complaining of his trials. He was coming to Timothy in tenderness and an inexplicable joy. He was modeling to Timothy and to us today, by example, that he is preparing him when saying anyone who wants to live a godly life in Christ Jesus will suffer persecution. It will come. There will be people who reject you, spit on your beliefs; there will be evil people and imposters who will flourish and be deceptive. Those kinds of people will be around. "But... you must stay faithful to the things that have been taught. You know they are true, for you know you can trust those who taught you. You have been taught the holy scriptures since childhood, and they have given you the wisdom to receive the salvation that comes by trusting in Christ Jesus. All scripture is inspired by God and is useful to teach us what is true and to make us realize what is wrong in our lives. It corrects us when we are wrong and teaches us to do what is right. God uses it to prepare and equip his people to do every good work" (2 Tim. 3:10-17 NLT).

Be thankful to the Lord for the work He is doing, even if it is not complete, even if it is painful today. Like so many before me, I look forward to meeting Paul. He endured the fires and trials, and he was thankful. Every time I read about him, I envision him being bruised and beaten yet overflowing with an inner joy and peace. He had such a deep, brotherly love for Timothy, and the way he talks to him is oozing with compassion and mercy. A thankful heart can't help but be merciful.

I was out with the bees, my miracle swarm, one perfect spring evening doing a hive check. They had just been transferred from the swarm trap the week before, and I did not know what to expect. I had my novice moments of panic in previous hive checks, but this time, I was determined to make friends with the bees and stay calm. I got my smoker going, zipped up my jacket, put on my gloves, and said a prayer before lifting the lid. Nothing could prepare me for the abundance of bees overflowing out of the frames. I stood there in awe for a moment, some panic pumping through my bloodstream, but there was an indescribable peace. It felt like a sacred moment standing there in the climactic buzz of nature with thousands of bees clouding above my head. I lifted a few frames and surprisingly spotted the queen quickly, but the number of bees was overwhelming. I accidentally squashed a few putting the frame back in, and that set off a domino effect of angry bees, a panicked beekeeper, and increasing volume of buzzing that resulted in a few stings. I calmly walked away this time as the guard bees settled back at their post. I slowly made my way back to the hive to close the lid when I noticed the few bees I had squashed were stumbling around on top. I realize beekeepers will inevitably squash some bees at times, but I felt horrible. I took great care of each bee and noticed one bee limping her way to a drop of honey. I watched her drink in her last meal and took in the sanctity of the moment. The Lord reminded me in the stillness of the beauty of life and the great care He takes for each life, that every life matters.

The Lord is close, closer than you may think or feel in this moment. He is a whisper away. "Be thankful in all things, for this is God's will for you who belong to Christ Jesus" (1 Thes. 5:18 NLT). We don't have to strive after God's will or search the world. We can be still and be thankful, for that is His will. When we start thanking Him and let our minds settle into the calm, we start to notice the honeybee drinking her last drop of honey and the woodpeckers poking for bugs, and we can't help but relish the moment.

What are you thankful for?

What makes you laugh?

What song comes to mind when you're doing a mindless chore?

Who are you thankful for?

**Action step #12.**

Write a list of fifty things you are thankful for. Write a letter to someone you're thankful for in your journal. Maybe you will decide to rip it out and mail it. Do you have an envelope and stamp? What joy that person would feel going to their mailbox and finding an actual written letter. Thankfulness is an exercise we practice. Philippians 4:9 says "practice these things" and then the God of peace will be with you. Set your mind on all that is good and then practice thankfulness today and every day.

# THANKFUL

## I'M THANKFUL FOR...

# BEE EVER-BLOOMING
## chapter 13

I was sitting in my college professor's office, crying over a breakup with a boyfriend. We were both in his ministry program under his counsel, and we were like oil and water always working through relational issues, but I sure was enthralled by him. My professor, Dr. C, said in a gentle voice right in a moment of pause when I needed to hear it most, "You are in a blooming process." I couldn't begin to know how these simple words of compassion would have such a profound, lasting effect on me and weave such an intricately designed picture of the Lord's work. The journey of faith is a slow, steady blooming and the Lord is never fully done with us. I'm speaking those words over you today, too.

You are in a blooming process, and the Lord is not done with you.

I think we overcomplicate God's will and purpose for our lives. He created us to make beautiful things in our own unique way and to share with others with a heart of thankfulness. He created us to bloom and grow, and share the love and mercy of Jesus with a light load in our backpack. The Lord doesn't want us to be weighed down with baggage, bogged down with bricks in our backpack. He wants to lighten our load so we can walk freely, enjoying each new day.

The wounds may still be there, but we can praise God for the wounds He has healed and the wounds He is still healing. We are all on a journey back to Eden, all with our own pain and struggles, stories to share and wounds we carry. No road is easier than another, and when we start to recognize the pain in others and see that Jesus was teaching us all along to consider others better than ourselves, our suffering starts to grow dim. "What joy for those whose strength comes from the Lord, who have set their minds on a pilgrimage to Jerusalem. When they walk through the Valley of Weeping it will become a place of refreshing springs. The autumn rains will clothe it with blessings. They will continue to grow stronger and each of them will appear before God in Jerusalem" (Psalm 84:5-6 NLT).

As we set our minds on the road ahead, we realize God will restore all things back to beauty and we will revel in the Garden of Eden. God reminds me, "Don't stay in the pit. Get back up and praise Me." He says, "Return to Me. You are still in the blooming process." This is what the Sovereign Lord, the Holy One of Israel says: "Only in returning to me and resting in me will you be saved. In quietness and confidence is your strength. But you would have none of it" (Isaiah 30:15 NLT). Back to the cross again where you first saw the Light. If we never had that experience of freedom with Jesus at the cross in the first place, how can we return to it in our times of despair? Have you experienced Jesus at the cross and seen the Light?

Would you have none of it or do you want to return to the Lord? Maybe you are tired of living in the puddle or going through the same motions at church. Maybe you feel like that smile you keep wearing is plastic. I have shared with you many of the intimate details in my heart. You know I'm not perfect and all the brokenness in my life is still not fully repaired, but in Christ, there is a way out. If you say you're doing all the things and still feeling stuck, let me ask you a question—have you been filled with the Holy Spirit? I'm not talking about the sweet Sunday school version of the fruits of the Spirit: love, joy, peace, patience, kindness, goodness, faithfulness, gentleness and self-control. That is who He is and the natural qualities we possess when we walk intimately with Him.

I'm talking about being a born-again believer, baptized in the Holy Spirit where He comes over you and consumes your heart giving you the ability to see the spiritual realm and be more aware of the spiritual battle going on in the unseen. "We are not fighting a battle against flesh and blood enemies, but against evil rulers and authorities of the unseen world, against mighty powers in this dark world and against evil spirits in the heavenly places" (Eph. 6:12 NLT). We have to be willing to do the spiritual work like Paul modeled for us so many times and believe there is rest for our weary souls even in the midst of trials and persecution.

If we believe the promises of God, we must persevere. "God's promise of entering His rest still stands" (Hebrews 4:1-2 NLT). When I was lying in my puddle feeling so ashamed, God was still there holding His hand out, saying His promise still stands and I can choose to grab hold. You can choose to take hold of His hand. "So, we ought to tremble with fear that some of you might fail to experience it. For this good news—that God has prepared this rest—has been announced to us just as it was to them, but it did them no good because they didn't share the faith of those who listened to God."

"For only we who believe can enter this rest." (Heb. 4:3 NLT)

For those who choose to stay in the puddle, God said, "In my anger I took an oath; they will never enter my place of rest. Even though this rest has been ready since he made the world, We know it is ready because of the place in the Scriptures where it mentions the seventh day; On the seventh day God rested from all His work. But in the other passage God said, they will never enter my place of rest. So, God's rest is there for people to enter, but those who first heard this good news failed to enter because they disobeyed God." (Heb. 4:3-6 NLT) God is offering His rest to you if you choose to obey and hear His voice. "So God set another time for entering His rest, and that time is today. God announced this through David much later in the words already quoted: Today when you hear His voice, don't harden your hearts." (Heb. 4:7 NLT)

"Now if Joshua had succeeded in giving them this rest, God would not have spoken about another day of rest still to come. So there is special rest still waiting for the people of God. For all who have entered into God's rest have rested from their labors, just as God did after creating the world. So let us do our best to enter that rest. But if we disobey God, as the people of Israel did, we will fall" (Heb. 4:8-11 NLT).

When we choose to enter into His rest, both today in this moment of turmoil and looking forward to the day when all the turmoil will be gone, we turn to God's Word where He opens our eyes to the words on the page and brings those words to light as if in neon letters. The words begin to jump off the page and breathe life back into the dullness of our hearts. Our souls begin to stir because God's word is alive and active. "For the word of God is alive and powerful. It is sharper than the sharpest two-edged sword, cutting between soul and spirit, between joint and marrow. It exposes our innermost thoughts and desires. Nothing in all creation is hidden from God. Everything is naked and exposed before His eyes, and He is the one to whom we are accountable." (Heb. 4:12-13 NLT)

When I was at my lowest point in my fast, my heart was stripped bare and pruned to a painful point of exposure. There was nothing left in me to hide. When I chose repentance, that is when His forgiveness consumed my heart. I could stand up and be free of the chains. I could see more clearly than I could in a long time.

The clouds parted and that stronghold couldn't cloud my mind any longer. When we choose to ignore God's voice and disobey His leading, that is when our hearts become hardened and the darkness grows darker and heavier. You can choose to drudge your way back up, distract your mind with your phone, drag your way to work. There are all kinds of distractions we can turn to as a way to keep our minds busy; it is easy to do, but God has so much more for you. More than you may be able to imagine or comprehend today. If you have read this far, you are a woman who doesn't want her ears to be tickled or to sit in your despair any longer. You want more of God. You know there is more, but maybe you don't know how to find the "more." It is closer than you may realize. Let's keep reading in Hebrews 4: "So then, since we have a great High Priest who has entered heaven, Jesus the Son of God, let us hold firmly to what we believe. This High Priest of ours understands our weaknesses, for he faced all the same testings we do, yet he did not sin. So let us come boldly to the throne of our gracious God. There we will receive his mercy, and we will find grace to help us when we need it most" (v. 14-15 NLT).

Notice the incredible beauty in that blooming process. We work to enter into His rest, we choose to enter His rest then He brings us to Scripture where He shows us our sins and weaknesses, but then He says He understands our weaknesses. He understands and He is still there holding His hand out. He is longing for us to take His hand and enter His rest. Then He says to choose Him, turn to Him and enter into the throne of grace with boldness. When we enter boldly, we will find mercy waiting for us. We will find grace to help us when we need it most.

When you groggily wake in the morning, feeling defeated before the day even begins and not wanting to face the day, you can choose to stay in that fog. Sometimes it truly is a mental fog that requires a knowledgeable person to help, but it could be a spiritual fog or a heavy soul where God is saying turn to Him and allow His work of the blooming process to take root in your heart. It seems the message of "choice" keeps coming through, but that is ultimately what God is teaching us. We have the choice daily to ignore His voice and deny the blessings He wants to pour on us or to choose Him. He longs for us to choose Him, to love Him with all our heart. Like the song "Come, Now is the Time to Worship," the greatest treasure remains for those who gladly choose Him. Are we gladly choosing Him?

We can choose to stay in our puddle, dwell on our torment and sufferings, and always trudge through each day. Or we can say, "I don't want this heavy, dark cloud anymore. Lord, show me in Your word, illuminate the words in Scripture and expose my innermost parts, baptize me in Your Holy Spirit and let me see the sin." That is where the work comes in. It is not fun or easy to do the work of exposing the darkness—we would rather stay hidden. We would rather stay behind the walls, locked in the cage, but God is saying, "Come out, take My hand and be free." He wants to walk with us through the blooming process so we don't stay the same. I never want to return to the darkness. But if Satan finds a foothold to bring me back to that dark place, I don't have to stay there. I don't have to feel ashamed that I crumbled again. I can get back up. Isaiah said, "Only in returning to me and resting in me will you be saved." (Is. 30:15 NLT). We can choose to return. We can always choose to return, and in returning to Him, He shows mercy, giving us grace and restores us. He is healing all those broken parts and growing loveliness in the blooming process.

It will be a process of perseverance every day until one day when all the blooming will build up and burst forth in a glorious display of Jesus returning. No one knows the day or the hour, not even Jesus. God's Word describes the events in Revelation, but there is no sense in troubling our minds with how it will happen before the tribulation, during, or after. God's people are urged to "endure persecution patiently, obeying His commands and maintaining their faith in Jesus" (Rev. 14:12 NLT) and to be ready for His return with our lights on.

It's all about Jesus.

We can't know all the mysteries and all knowledge, but we can turn to the One who does, the One who has conquered death, who triumphs over all darkness in the end. We may not know how to get out of our puddle today, but we know the One who can lift us out. We don't have to know all the answers, but we can cling to the One who does know. The glory of the gospel is the blooming process of His mercy and the glorious unveiling of Jesus our Messiah. We can say it's all about Jesus.

Just Jesus.

Have you been to the foot of the cross and seen the Light of Jesus?

How have your burdens been lifted?

Are you seeing Jesus is who truly matters?

Are you seeing that YOU matter to Him?

**Action Step #13**

Rest your mind. Be still. Write out your testimony (that's a fancy word for story) of what Jesus means to you. There will be a time to share it with someone who needs to hear it. Let inspiration flow freely. If you were in my brain right now I'm envisioning a field of wildflowers with bees buzzing everywhere and I would be writing a verse that is meaningful to me right now, or writing a piece to share and I'd be pulling out the colored pencils to make it bright and colorful. You have a story of blooming beauty that only you can share in your own unique way and the Lord wants you to share it.

These bees are cleaning up some broken honeycomb. We all have our individual role and part to play.

# BLOOMING
*beauty*

TAKE THE HAND OF JESUS AND WALK WITH HIM. HE IS BY YOUR SIDE AND STICKS CLOSER THAN A BROTHER.

## WHAT IS YOUR STORY?

YOU ARE IN A BLOOMING PROCESS.

# chapter 14

Tangerines have become a simple reminder of God's presence and faithfulness in our lives. The day we moved onto the property, our neighbor gave us a basket overflowing with tangerines from her fruit trees as a welcome and told us they were symbolic of abundance. Farm life is our life now. It is small but it's ever-blooming with seasons of gray dormancy and seasons of bright, abundant life. We raised our sweet rooster, named Tangerine, from our first batch of incubated eggs and he is our last lonely chicken wandering around the farm. After many attacks, hens reaching old age, and butchering, he has become our family pet. We will bring our rooster more friends to the farm and raise more hens for him to protect, but for today, he carries on pecking and scratching. The gardens are pruned back, plants are shriveled and brown. It rains most days in this season but the light frost in the mornings are a respite after the scorching summer months. The bees are cuddled up and cozy in their hives, and it's a season of lull as we anticipate new life. Did you know honey can stay preserved for hundreds of years? If it is produced and capped the way God designed.

We can have joyful and abundant lives if we walk out our faith the way God designed. Living by faith each day is not copying the behavior of this world but letting God transform us into a new person by changing the way we think, then we will know God's will for us which is good and pleasing and perfect (Rom.12:2 NLT). We can experience His perfect will if we listen to what He says and do what it says (James 1:22 NLT). It is simply stepping out of the boat and moving toward Jesus–a simple step but it's not easy. Peter was the only disciple of twelve who did step out and walk on water. If it was easy maybe all the disciples would have been running toward Jesus. Think about the scene for a moment. It's raging storms, strong winds, heavy waves that must have been crashing over their boat, terror settling over their minds and they see a figure out on the water. They assume it's a ghost and Peter is the only one who spoke up in faith asking to come out to Jesus walking on the water. He was the only one to step out toward Jesus. A step that required great faith (Matt. 14:22-33 NLT). Peter could have waited for his friends to step out first or maybe they were telling him he was crazy for stepping out and he could have stayed safe in the boat. He didn't seem to hesitate or look at them before going forward in faith. I have a tendency to look to people or need affirmation before stepping out. If they have faith to step out then I can too. None of us want to look weird alone but even when Peter was sinking, he could have looked back at his friends hoping they would reach out to save him, instead he looked to Jesus. I tend to look back to people in the storms of my life hoping they will come to my rescue, but we see through Peter's example that our eyes should be fixed on Jesus at every moment of the storm and go forward in faith. He was walking out his own personal faith not listening to the disciples in the boat or looking at them when he was sinking. He didn't walk without stumbling, he still had a moment of doubt and Jesus reached out his hand. "You have so little faith," Jesus said. "Why did you doubt me?" (Matt. 14:31 NLT) Immediately after that the wind stopped. We can trust Jesus. Our feet can falter and he will be there to catch us. Walking out our faith is being present with the Lord each moment, fixing our eyes on Him and following His leading each day.

We can stay safe inside the boat or sit safe in the pew and keep our seat warm but being a disciple of Jesus means stepping out in faith even when the storms are raging around us. Sometimes we will be by ourselves and we'll look weird but that is your personal faith journey with Jesus. Peter most likely shared the incredible story after that day of how he walked on water in the middle of a storm and Jesus saved him, wouldn't you want to share that story? When we encounter Jesus we can't contain our joy bubbling up to share the stories of His goodness. There is power in sharing stories. "And they have defeated him by the blood of the lamb, and by their testimony. And they did not love their lives so much that they were afraid to die" (Revelation 12:11 NLT). There is power over darkness to defeat the Enemy by sharing our testimony and sharing what the Lord has done. The roots of a tree take some time to germinate deep in the soil before the sapling can begin to sprout. It's okay to sit for a while and let our roots grow deep in the Lord, but at some point in our journey, we must get up out of our seats and start sharing what the Lord has done. We will want to share. We will want to step out of the boat on our own. Peter asked Jesus if it was really him and he went out. We must grow in maturity and follow where He leads. "Just as the body is dead without breath, so also faith is dead without good works" (James 2:26 NLT).

There are action steps the Lord is asking you to take if you are willing to obey and let Him lead the way. I put my faith in Jesus, and He set me free on the cross. That was only the first step. But then I went on this weaving, winding path for several years, wondering why I didn't feel free. I was still tripping so easily on every rock, falling back into old patterns and into the darkness of my mind battles. I wondered why I kept seeing rotten fruit come out of my heart and realized I wasn't dealing with the root issue. It is not pleasant to be around people who produce rotten fruit. They are not a ray of sunshine. I have been that person. I have been stuck in seasons of my life, hitting the same rock that wasn't breaking. Finally, the Lord brought me to the end of myself, and I cried out to Him, "What do I have to do? I'll do anything!"

Would I really do anything? Was I willing to do a forty-day fast like Jesus? That seemed daunting, and I had small children at home depending on me. There are only a few times in scripture forty-day fasts are mentioned, but I was desperate. This lifelong battle of mental torment didn't seem to be going away. The practical step the Lord was leading me to was forty days of femininity. You won't find that anywhere in the Bible, but God is not in a box, and His ways can be creative in the way He speaks to us individually. He is a personal God and knows us more intimately than we know ourselves. He continually teaches me that we find true freedom in the daily disciplines, and I was not disciplined. I was aimless and lacking in direction.

As lovely as it would be if we could be like caterpillars taking a nice long nap while they metamorphose and come out flying, God formed us as human beings to become like Him, reflecting His character in the sanctification process. We must take steps to grow in maturity. Was I willing to put in the action steps of obedience? Or was I still being stubborn? I was determined to develop discipline and a sound mind (2 Tim. 1:7 NLT) that could stand against the Enemy. He most certainly will keep slinking around looking for any crack to sneak into for the rest of our days, but God does give us armor to put on (Eph. 6:10 NLT). He gives us tools to use and leads us to the right tool for the right time if we are searching His Word for help. I knew what the Lord was asking me to do—get up, make my bed, put on a dress and a splash of color. He was asking me to get disciplined and train my mind, rooting myself daily in His Word and being consistent for forty days. I have always been striving to follow Jesus since I asked Him into my heart at four years old. Some would even say I appeared to be a put-together mom, wife, and Godly woman, but deep under the surface, there was rot I didn't want to confront. It is my personal tendency to fall into laziness and slump through the morning; starting the day too late then the whole day is set back.

One morning, I woke up with no more excuses. The battles in the night had gone on long enough, the mental pit of despair was too deep to fight on my own strength, and I couldn't go on any longer. I found my will to fight, but not in my own efforts that inevitably fell flat. I was ready to set my mind on God's truth and align my heart with His, so began the forty days of femininity to discipline myself with new rhythms and new mindsets. Culture tells women to rise above and try harder, but Scripture tells women to put on the fine linen and represents a righteous act (Revelation 19:8 NIV). If we are doing that righteous act in humility and obedience, God is faithful to produce purity and loveliness in us. He is going to develop noble character and be clothed in strength and dignity (Proverbs 31:25a NLT) as we put our faith in Him. King Lemuel's mother taught her son to live to a higher standard and to look for a wife of noble character; she is more precious than rubies (Proverbs 31:10 NLT). The fruit of these inner qualities comes out as we become more like Christ. This kind of woman is feminine and modest. She is set apart from the ways of this world and lives to a higher standard dressing the part–both in obedience and willingness. She dresses in fine linen and purple gowns (Prov. 31:22 NLT).

Each day I faithfully got up and took one step forward, and God faithfully met me there. I started to notice an emerging pattern with red, then orange the next day, and yellow, green, blue, purple, violet. It turned into a seven day pattern of the rainbow. It spoke of His promises. He would speak to me through colors in nature. The Lord is so personal with us. He showed me His heart for femininity and His original design to walk intimately close with Him like Adam and Eve did in the garden of Eden. Every lesson I noticed was popping out from the gardens and hearing His words of truth ringing in my ears. That still, small voice was becoming clearer and more understandable every day, a song or a verse would come to mind. The way I dressed directly influenced the rhythm of my day and my frame of mind in how I approached home life. My attitude toward homeschool lessons was more productive; meals were prepared with more ease. I didn't feel slouchy and lazy. The Lord was molding me and making me new. I was becoming a more beautiful creation as I was walking intimately with the Creator. I even bought a  linen dress and it was purple! If you feel compelled to do a similar forty-day commitment, I encourage you to search God's word for yourself. He will show you the area He wants to grow in you and bring you to the passage that is right for the time.

All my life I have heard, "read your Bible, pray, journal." Those are all the right things to do and good daily disciplines, yes; however, if it is just a box to check, it won't be meaningful or produce growth. If we truly want to be untangled from the wounds and strongholds, there are further resources that can lead us to victory and freedom. A good place to start may be the book *Understanding the Wounded Heart* by Marcus Warner. It walks you through practical counseling steps to acknowledge your wounds while pouring your heart out to God as your Counselor.

God's Word is enough. We are not to add to or take away from it. "So be careful to obey all the commands I give you. You must not add anything to them or subtract anything from them" (Deut. 12:32 NLT). We can walk the path to total freedom with God's Word alone. Jesus said, "I am the Bread of Life. Whoever comes to me will never go hungry, and whoever believes in me will never go thirsty" (John 6:35 NLT). When we are stumbling around in a dark season or tangled in despair, we don't always know where to read in Scripture. I understand being surrounded by a heavy cloud and stuck in the fog of our own mind. But we do have a Helper—the Holy Spirit is our faithful guide to lead us, even to the right place in scripture. There are times when He will lead us to a helpful book or a friend, a mentor, or a stranger on a park bench might nudge us back in the right direction. And it is always Scripture, no matter how far we have veered off the path. What matters is that God is pursuing your heart. He will find you in the words on a page or an item at the thrift store. When we start noticing the rotten fruit coming out of our heart, we can turn to Him for help, and He will work on our heart. That heart work can hurt, but if we spend some time reading the book of Hebrews chapters two through five, we see the author calling the believers out of darkness into living in the light and to grow in spiritual maturity.

He is urging us, as brothers and sisters, "to make sure our own hearts are not evil and unbelieving, turning you away from the living God" (Heb. 3:12 NLT). He follows that with assurance that we will share in all that belongs to Christ if we are faithful. Do you trust God just as firmly as the day you first believed (Heb. 3:14 NLT)? Go back to your first love, and keep a soft teachable heart. He warns us not to harden our hearts. The Israelites who did are scattered in the wilderness. Their unbelief kept them from entering rest. He says, "So we see that *because of their unbelief* they were not able to enter his rest" (Heb. 3:19 NLT). Unbelief is an unforgivable sin. Unbelief separates us from God. It is the wall between us and freedom. God was angry with the Israelites when they repeatedly hardened their hearts and would not believe. They could not enter his rest. They witnessed miracles and saw the glory of God yet still rebelled and hardened their hearts. Paul goes on to share God's promise of entering His rest. We can still enter that rest in fear and trembling. That offer is still for us today.

If we are listening and taking the faithful, steady, practical steps of believing in His promises, we can enter His rest (Heb. 4:2-3 NLT). If we are ready and want to get right with the Lord, we can get all we need straight from scripture. "Nothing in all creation is hidden from God. Everything is naked and exposed before his eyes, and he is the one to whom we are accountable" (Heb. 4:13 NLT). God already knows what you are struggling with; He knows what you need and where to lead you. You just have to be willing and ask. That can feel too broad, "just ask," but let's read on. The author of Hebrews is again saying "hold firmly to what we believe." It says back in chapter two that Jesus was like us; He became flesh and blood. Then again in chapter four: "he understands our weaknesses, for he faced all the same testings we do, yet he did not sin." The action steps He is calling you to do by faith, believing He will meet you, is to "come boldly to the throne of our gracious God." You can take an actual step and come to a place of prayer, to the altar, to speak the actual words to a friend, "I need prayer." Boldly move out of your seat and break the silence. Take that step to deepen your faith. "There we will receive mercy, and we will find grace to help us when we need it most" (Heb.4:16 NLT). He says "there." One step out of your comfort zone and God promises to meet you there. He can sit with you in your seat, in the silence of your despair. He can comfort you there and offer to walk alongside you, but unless you take a step of action, your faith will stay dead. There won't be any change, any transformation, or any beautifully painted butterfly flying free. God longs to heal your broken wing, but you have to take the steps He is asking you to take and trust Him. He promises rest, but you have to have the faith and action to enter. If you want a day of true rest, no chores piled up, you have to do the work the day before and prepare for the day of rest. It takes intentional effort to enter rest. "O Lord, do good to those who are good, whose hearts are in tune with you" (Psalm 125:4 NLT).

The book of Hebrews calls us to spiritual growth later in chapter five. We can choose to stay spiritually dull and not listen, but we are urged to a higher calling, to move on to the solid food and become mature in our understanding. We can live on milk our whole life and stay infants, but God has so much more for us to become. If you know the basics, you have already repented of the sin in your heart and put your faith in Jesus. If you have asked God to search you and know your heart (Psalm 139:23-24 NLT), then He will be faithful to lead you into maturity. Tune your heart to Him, sing a hymn and pray scripture. He doesn't want to see you sitting stagnant in the same suffering your whole life. Jesus didn't hang on the cross so you could stay the same. Confess your sin, ask Him to cancel your debt, and command the evil spirits to leave in Jesus' name. There is power in the name Jesus. We can resist Satan and his demons, and they have to flee in Jesus' name (James 4:7 NLT). The truth to see is that darkness cannot exist in the light, and Jesus is the Light.

"God is light, and there is no darkness in Him at all. So we are lying if we say we have fellowship with God but go on living in spiritual darkness; we are not practicing the truth. But if we are living in the light, as God is in the light, then we have fellowship with each other, and the blood of Jesus cleanses us from all sin" (1 John 1:5-7 NLT). Lying is a powerful choice word. We are lying if we say our faith is in the cleansing blood of Jesus but then choose to continue living in darkness. We are lying to ourselves and we are deceived if we are not willing to confess those self-sins; sins of despair, sins of unbelief, sins of demonic oppression. We can take steps toward Jesus and allow Him who is Light to expose the darkness. Sing the name Jesus if that is all you can muster, and the darkness will fade. It won't be gone completely unless you confront the root issue and commit to replacing it with God's truth, but the darkness will flee. His desire for you is to continue growing and transforming.

When rotten fruit comes flying out of your mouth, ask yourself where it is coming from and bring it boldly to the throne room. When you return to an old habit, ask God what you need to do to pluck that rotten root out and replace it with healthy nutrients. It could be a certain kind of fast or a commitment He is asking you to obey. If you wake up every morning and can't bear to face another day, it may be a deeper issue that needs to be confronted with a God-fearing Christian counselor. Someone who will walk with you into the depths of heart issues and with the help of the Holy Spirit you can find deliverance. There can be generational strongholds that need to be broken. It could be addictions that won't relent. It could be a lie you can trace back to the elementary school playground or a wound you can trace back to a broken relationship. There is nothing hidden from God, remember. All is naked and exposed. That "thing" you cling to so tightly hiding in the darkness feels impossible to ever break free from. I'm here to tell you it is possible. It is very possible.

If there is nothing in your darkness that would scare me away or a secret that would shock me, just imagine what your loving and holy Heavenly Father would do when you take that step of faith into His arms. He is waiting for you with arms wide open, my friend. Just breathe and take that step. Grab hold of His hand. Then keep taking the steps He leads you to take, and little by little, all those tangled up knots are going to loosen. Sometimes releasing strongholds can be instantaneous, and you will wonder why you couldn't make that step sooner. Other times, the day comes and we didn't even realize God was healing our heart all along.

"If we claim we have no sin, we are only fooling ourselves and not living in the truth. But if we confess our sins to him, he is faithful and just to forgive us our sins and cleanses us from all wickedness. If we claim we have not sinned, we are calling God a liar and showing that his word has no place in our hearts" (1 John 1:8-9 NLT).

If we continue to choose sin or wallow in self-pity, we are showing we have no place for Him in our hearts and may as well give in to Satan's schemes. We don't want that or we wouldn't still be here reading.

"My dear children, I am writing this to you so that you will not sin. But if anyone does sin, we have an advocate who pleads our case before the Father. He is Jesus Christ, the one who is truly righteous. He Himself is the sacrifice that atones for our sins—and not only our sins but the sins of all the world. And we can be sure that we know Him if we obey His commandments. If someone claims, 'I know God,' but doesn't obey God's commandments, that person is a liar and is not living in the truth. But those who obey God's word truly show how completely they love Him. That is how we know we are living in Him. Those who say they live in God should live their lives as Jesus did" (1 John 2:1-6 NLT). We can spend our whole lives running and never slow down long enough to know Him. He wants you to know Him and to let yourself be fully known by Him. We can gain all the head knowledge in the world and never see Jesus. If we are a disciple of Jesus learning from Him, we should be living as He did.

Satan wants to keep non-believers blind and keep believers in bondage but Jesus shows a way out. We want freedom from Satan's snares and schemes, and that means loving God's Word and obeying it. Others will know we love God if we obey His commandments. When we sin, we have an Advocate who pleads our case before the Father. We are women who get back up, and when it feels like all we are doing is falling and getting back up, or falling and can't get back up, that is a check in our spirit to go to our heavenly Father for help. The steps of faith He leads us to take should be producing growth, joy, freedom and living as Jesus did. The more I see my own sin or my old patterns of living in darkness, the more I want to turn to God's truth to change. He is after a much bigger purpose, He is after our heart and growing us to become more like Jesus. I want to keep growing, keep blooming, keep moving forward with nothing hindering me or weighing me down—doesn't that sound wonderful?

At the mention of the name Jesus, darkness flees, oppression lifts, hearts melt, bitterness withers. There is no darkness in Him at all. There may be weeping in the night, but joy comes in the morning (Ps. 30:5 NLT). We can dance, we can sing, we can worship our God because He set us free. Glory to God, He has set us free. Turn on that old hymn and let yourself just thank the Lord for what He has done. He took our chains and our bondage so we could not just be free in eternity but that we could live free and forgiven today. You don't have to believe the lie that you will just suffer in sin your whole life. The more we look to Jesus, the more we will be satisfied. We will have a healed heart, ready to say "Here I am Lord I'll go where You send me." We will be more willing to take actual steps across the street to a neighbor or across the field to hug a friend.

Don't be afraid to come out into the light.

Don't be afraid to communicate your areas of brokenness and get the healing you need. All the tools we need are right in front of us, right in God's Word, like treasures waiting to be found. Don't be afraid to do the hard work so you can be that healthy, lovely woman of strength and dignity, ready to be that friend to others that you want them to be for you. In a world that is more connected yet more lonely than ever, we need each other and we need to be strong in the Lord for what may come. Simply noticing someone else and showing interest in their life is living as Jesus did. God designed us to know and be known, both by our Heavenly Father and the family of believers. We can learn to be better friends, wives, mothers, daughters, and sisters as our faith grows deeply rooted in the truth of God's word. Be right with the Lord and ready for His return. Go out and live as Jesus did with a sense of urgency to make disciples of all nations. The Lord promises to be with you always, even to the end of the age (Matt. 28:19-20 NLT). The road back to Eden is the narrow way and it isn't the easy way but you have a purpose. "Don't be afraid of suffering for the Lord. Work at telling others the Good News, and fully carry out the ministry God has given you" (2 Tim. 4:5 NLT). He has given you a special role to fulfill in His plan even if that means stepping out alone. He will light the way as you move forward. Simply trust Him.

When we start to really see all His goodness and how deep, how vast, how great His love is, that is when we start to see the beauty in the honey that He was producing all along. *Bee* a wild woman with great faith, rooted deeply in the truth of Jesus. It's your turn to take the next step of faith and see where the Lord leads. Buy yourself a purple dress, bloom into the woman God made you to be and believe you are set free.

# WE CAN ALWAYS RUN TO JESUS

## CLING TO GOD'S PROMISES FOUND IN SCRIPTURE.

## BEE A WILD WOMAN WITH GREAT FAITH, ROOTED DEEPLY IN THE TRUTH OF JESUS.

"THE GRASS WITHERS AND THE FLOWERS FADE BUT THE WORD OF THE LORD IS ETERNAL."
ISAIAH 40:8

# acknowledgments

It is hearts of thankfulness that make us strong, and I am beyond thankful for each person who was a special piece in putting this puzzle together!

This book was stirring in my heart for many years, and it felt nothing more than a distant dream until I met my publisher, Katie Zeliger, who believed my story mattered and took a chance on me. Thank you for doing such a wonderful job bringing these words to life and designing artwork that far exceeded my expectations. Every decision is very evidently Holy Spirit breathed. Your patience and professionalism along the journey helped me as a first-time author to grow as a writer. You truly are a gem. From the bottom of my heart: THANK YOU!!

To my editors, Wyeth and Leah, thank you for all the critiques, your attention to detail, and for putting your time into my passion project. Ironically, grammar was never my strength, and you helped me organize my thoughts and find the words to make it the best possible book it could be. I am forever grateful to you.

Mom and Dad, thank you for faithfully bringing me to church and pointing me to Jesus. You had faith in my writing long before anyone else and lit the spark in my heart that made me believe a book was possible.

My dear friends and sisters in Christ, thank you for supporting me along the way!! Jess N., thank you for being the true friend who gave me the kick in the pants I needed to take this book seriously and challenged me to obey where God was leading. You poured into the pages with me and always genuinely cared. Farran S., thank you for being my cheerleader in the low points and praying me through; you were a godsend. Kara L., thank you for being a listening ear. Your lifelong friendship is a cherished treasure! Paige M., you always thought to call and check-in, and your vibrant faith (and fashion) brings joy to my day. Jamie C., your encouragement was a breath of fresh air when the days felt long; thank you for sticking with me. Abbi G., your desire to grow deeper in your faith spurs me on; the miles are far between us, but our hearts are close. And lastly, to my sister Lisa D., you showed up when I needed you most; your ministry of presence filled my heart more than you will ever know. Thank you for taking the time to notice and consider me.

To all my kids, one day you'll see just how deep my love for you goes and come to know there is a good God who loves you even more. You played a part in building His kingdom by helping make this book become a reality. You always considered your mama, knocked on my door to ask if I needed anything, and kept my water cup full. You kept me going!!

And to my most favorite person in all the world, my husband Sam, you gave me the courage to send my wild heart into the world. You have been my best friend through the years; you persevered with me and have always been by my side. This book wouldn't exist if it weren't for you lovingly pulling me back up every time I fell into doubt. You are such an example of steady, unwavering faith. Thank you for your constant support and self-less love, no matter what. I choose you today and every day.

My deepest heart of gratitude to my Savior Jesus Christ. He paid it all, and all to him I owe.

# meet the author

Heidi Hinnenkamp is a follower of Jesus Christ and loves to dig through God's word for the hidden treasures. After attending Trinity International University to study Counseling, she began writing to encourage others to notice beauty among the thorns of life and to go deeper in their walk with the Lord. Heidi enjoys a slower paced life in the Lowcountry of South Carolina with her husband Sam and their six children.

You can connect with her via email beautyinhoney@gmail.com or find her on Instagram @bee_rooted_farm

www.ingramcontent.com/pod-product-compliance
Lightning Source LLC
Chambersburg PA
CBHW070705130626
46553CB00005B/1846